Handel

The Complete Series

Bach *Tim Dowley*
Bartók *Hamish Milne*
Beethoven *Ates Orga*
Berlioz *Robert Clarson-Leach*
Brahms *Paul Holmes*
Chopin *Ates Orga*
Debussy *Paul Holmes*
Dvořák *Neil Butterworth*
Elgar *Simon Mundy*
Gilbert & Sullivan *Alan James*
Handel *Wendy Thompson*
Haydn *Neil Butterworth*
Liszt *Bryce Morrison*
Mahler *Edward Seckerson*
Mendelssohn *Mozelle Moshansky*
Mozart *Peggy Woodford*
Offenbach *Peter Gammond*
Paganini *John Sugden*
Prokofiev *David Gutman*
Rachmaninoff *Robert Walker*
Ravel *David Burnett-James*
Rossini *Nicholas Till*
Schubert *Peggy Woodford*
Schumann *Tim Dowley*
Shostakovich *Eric Roseberry*
Sibelius *David Burnett-James*
Strauss Family *Peter Kemp*
Strauss (Richard) *David Nice*
Tchaikovsky *Wilson Strutte*
Verdi *Peter Southwell-Sander*
Villa-Lobos *Lisa Peppercorn*
Vivaldi *John Booth*
Wagner *Howard Gray*
Weber *Anthony Friese-Greene*

The Illustrated Lives of the Great Composers.

Handel

Wendy Thompson

OMNIBUS PRESS
LONDON · NEW YORK · SYDNEY

Cover design and art direction by Studio Twenty London
Cover photography by Julian Hawkins
Text design by David Morley-Clarke

© Wendy Thompson 1994
This edition published in 1994 by Omnibus Press, a division of Book Sales Limited

Order No. OP46796
ISBN 0.7119.2997.1

Exclusive Distributors:
Book Sales Limited,
8/9 Frith Street,
London W1V 5TZ, England

Music Sales Corporation
257 Park Avenue South
New York, NY10010, USA

Music Sales Pty Ltd.,
120 Rothschild Avenue,
Rosebery, NSW 2018, Australia

To the Music Trade only:
Music Sales Limited,
8/9 Frith Street,
London WIV 5TZ, England

Typeset by DMC Design Associates, London
Printed and bound in the UK by
Staples Printers Rochester Limited,
Neptune Close, Medway City Estate, Frindsbury,
Rochester, Kent ME2 4LT

Contents

Introduction   7

1   Halle   13

2   Hamburg   23

3   Italy   31

4   Music and Culture in Queen Anne's London   49

5   Early Years in London   60

6   Cannons   72

7   The Royal Academy of Music   83

8   From Opera to Oratorio   103

Interlude: The Man   125

9   New Directions   134

10   *Messiah*   146

11   *Music for the Royal Fireworks*   160

12   'Total eclipse'   170

Selected List of Works   182

Selected Bibliography   186

Acknowledgements and References   188

Index   189

Introduction

The distinction due to Shakespeare in energy of poetry, to Michelangelo in sculpture and painting, Handel may justly claim in the sister art; to him belongs the Majesty of Music. The merit of Handel is not confined; it is of universal cast, that he may be styled the great musician of nature.

In the summer of 1750, the remains of Johann Sebastian Bach were quietly laid to rest in St John's cemetery in Leipzig. He left a modest estate, a widow who spent the rest of her life in dire poverty, and a musical legacy that lay neglected and largely unperformed for nearly 80 years. Nine years later, three thousand mourners crowded into Westminster Abbey to witness the 'private' burial of Bach's fellow-countryman and exact contemporary, George Frideric Handel, whose reputation – especially in his adopted country – suffered no such eclipse.

In 1784, in the mistaken belief that they were celebrating the centenary of his birth (they were, in fact, one year early), a group of Handel's most enthusiastic admirers conceived the idea of a series of commemoration performances in the Abbey, 'on such a scale of magnificence, as could not be equalled in any part of the world'. The great aisle was converted into an auditorium hung with crimson damask; while the royal box was festooned with gold-fringed white satin. By 9.00am on 26 May, the front door of Westminster Abbey was besieged by 'such a croud of ladies and gentlemen...as became very formidable and terrific to each other'. King George III personally insisted that the event should be extended 'to three days instead of two, which he thought would not be sufficient for the display of HANDEL's powers', wrote the official chronicler, Dr Charles Burney: and so for each concert – first a selection from Handel's anthems and oratorios, then a programme of Italian and English arias and instrumental music, and finally, a complete performance of *Messiah* – the organisers assembled some 513 performers, 'a more numerous band than was ever known to be collected in any country, or on

A view of the choir and orchestra in Westminster Abbey during the Handel Commemoration in 1784.

7

The orchestral seating plan for the 1784 celebrations.

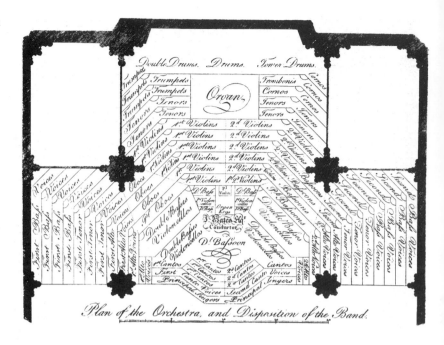

Plan of the Orchestra, and Disposition of the Band.

any occasion whatever'. This massive orchestra incorporated 'every species of instrument that was capable of producing grand effects', including six trombones, a double bassoon, and the 'Double-Base Kettle Drums…more capacious than the common kettle-drum'. 'The effect of the first crash of such a band' was astonishing. 'Wonder mixed with pleasure appeared in every countenance', wrote an observer. 'So many voices, such prodigious kettle drums, that most powerfull instrument the trombone and the loftiness of the place…all conspired to make the choruses at the Church grand indeed.' 'The immense volume and torrent of sound was almost too much for the head or the senses to bear – we were elevated into a species of delirium', reported the *European Magazine*.

   The success of the first Handel Commemoration, which raised six thousand pounds for charity, encouraged further repetitions, each bigger and grander than the last: in 1786, 640 performers were so 'thunderfull' that they gave Horace Walpole a headache; by 1791, when Haydn attended *Messiah*, the numbers had swollen to 1,068. By then, Burney, who privately considered that the excessive British idolatry of Handel had 'prevented us from keeping pace with the rest of Europe in the cultivation of Music', was openly suggesting that the Commemorations had had their day: 'It cannot reasonably be supposed, that there is a sufficient number of persons in this kingdom, whose wealth, or zeal for the honour of this great and famous master, will continue much longer to enable or incline them to attend such an expensive performance year after year, merely to hear the same pieces

The 1859 Handel Festival held at Crystal Palace.

repeated.' None-the-less, the tradition of 'monster performances' resumed at the beginning of Queen Victoria's reign, and continued unabated through the nineteenth century, while adulation of Handel reached a new pitch of fervour. In 1857, the Grand Handel Festival was transferred from Westminster Abbey to Crystal Palace, built for the Great Exhibition in Hyde Park and reassembled on a hill in Sydenham. A 'wonderful assembly of 2,000 vocal and 500 instrumental performers' gave three oratorios, while the Queen was observed to beat time with a fan. Two years later, the combined choir and orchestra had swollen to 3,225, while in 1883, 4,500 performers entertained an audience of nearly 88,000. The tradition of 'Handel Festivals' survived even the First World War: the last took place in 1926 at Crystal Palace. Handel had become a national institution, such performances an excuse for demonstrations of national solidarity and patriotism.

Handel's music was revered not only in England. Few composers have exerted such widespread influence on the mainstream of European music. Mozart re-orchestrated *Acis and Galatea, Messiah, From harmony* and *Alexander's Feast* to suit late-eighteenth-century Viennese taste; Haydn considered the chorus 'The Nations tremble at the dreadful sound' (from *Joshua*) a 'sublime composition', and took Handelian models for his own oratorios *The Creation* and *The Seasons*; while Beethoven, who, in 1796, wrote a set of variations on 'See, the conqu'ring hero comes', told a friend shortly before his death that in future, he would write each year 'in the manner of my grand-master Handel

9

only an oratorio or a string or wind concerto'. In the 1830s, the young Mendelssohn conducted performances of Handel's oratorios in Düsseldorf, and paid him the compliment of imitation in his own *St Paul* and *Elijah*.

Meanwhile, the Handel industry was gathering momentum. John Mainwaring's *Memoirs of the Life of the late George Frederic Handel*, the first composer biography, appeared in 1760; while 25 years later, Samuel Arnold opened a subscription for a complete edition of Handel's works – the first attempt at a *Gesamtausgabe*. George III ordered 25 copies, but the project foundered, and it was left to the German Handel Society, under the direction of the musicologist Friedrich Chrysander, to pick up the pieces in the mid-nineteenth century. (Handel's numerous revisions, adaptations and additions flummoxed both Arnold and, eventually, even the indefatigable Chrysander; and a new complete edition, the *Hallische Händel Ausgabe*, was inaugurated in 1955.)

The key to Handel's immense popularity lay in his unique ability to soak up stylistic influences, extract their essence, and synthesise them into a personal style which reflected – in a single *oeuvre* – the best features of Baroque music. Through his experiences at Hamburg, he learnt about orchestration from Keiser, and came into contact with the French style of Lully, which not only enabled him later to reproduce French-style ballet sequences for the dancer Marie Sallé, but to absorb Lully's dramatic handling of the subject-matter of *tragédie-lyrique* – whether magical or historical (several of Handel's most popular operas were based on texts formerly set by Lully). In Italy, he learnt from Corelli how to write for strings, and from Alessandro Scarlatti how to handle Italian vocal techniques; while from the legacy of Purcell and his contemporaries he learnt how to set English words, and borrowed the ceremonial style which stood him in such good stead for his own royal commissions.

Nevertheless, had Handel remained steadfast to his first love, *opera seria*, he would doubtless have suffered the same fate as his contemporary and fellow-countryman Hasse – acclaimed in his lifetime as the best opera composer in Europe – but subsequently relegated to the pages of text-books as an interesting historical figure. Once *opera seria* had fallen out of fashion in the mid-eighteenth century, Handel's own works, the apotheosis of Baroque opera, were forgotten for nearly two centuries. Interest in them was first revived in Germany in the 1920s; but failed to take root in England until the mid-1950s, with the formation of the Handel Opera Society. Since then, despite the rapid growth of period-instrument ensembles, the technical problems and sheer expense of staging Baroque opera have prevented Handel's *oeuvre* from becoming widely known until very recently, when

several notable revivals and complete recordings of some lesser-known operas and oratorios have lifted the lid off an inexhaustible treasure trove.

Handel's creative survival – even during his lifetime – depended on his ability to transfuse the lifeblood of a dying art-form – *opera seria* – into a living one – the English oratorio. A man of the theatre, he seized on the dramatic possibilities inherent in Old Testament tales of heroism and sacrifice. Tedious *da capo* arias, designed to show off the technique of the Italian *prime donne*, were largely abandoned in favour of more concise, fluently melodious airs in *arioso* style, while the spotlight was turned on the chorus, to enhance moments of terror by sheer weight of sound; to depict in vivid word-painting – assisted by apt and occasionally exotic orchestral scoring – natural or supernatural phenomena such as the plagues of insects or hailstones which afflict Egypt (*Israel in*

11

Egypt), the fall of the walls of Jericho, or the sun standing still (*Joshua*). The drama was inherent in the music: no elaborate scenic effects or stage properties were needed. By transferring the exclusivity of the stage to the all-embracing ambit of the concert hall, Handel unknowingly fulfilled the aspirations of future generations of middle-class music-lovers and amateur singers, who enjoy taking part in an essentially dramatic production without the accompanying tension of solo rôles or stage appearances. From 1846 onwards, the issue of cheap vocal scores of the oratorios by the enterprising firm of Novello brought first-hand experience of Handel's music to England's flourishing choral societies, since which time it has formed the backbone of their repertory, a treasured part of the national musical heritage. Wagner qualified the nature of the English response to Handel on hearing *Messiah* in London in 1855:

It was here that I began to comprehend the true spirit of English musical culture, which is closely allied to the spirit of English Protestantism. This accounts for the fact that an oratorio is more attractive to the public than an opera. The audience has the advantage of feeling that an evening spent listening to an oratorio is like a kind of service, and is nearly as good as going to church. Everyone holds a Handel vocal score as if it were a prayer-book.

It is none-the-less one of the ironies of music history that, while the latter-day 'Bach revival' should have encouraged the performance, broadcasting and recording of all Bach's major works, both vocal and instrumental, Handel's posthumous reputation has until recently rested on a handful of pieces – the *Water Music* and *Fireworks Music*, the most popular oratorios, especially *Messiah*, the *concerti grossi*, and one or two individual instrumental pieces, such as *The Harmonious Blacksmith*. Yet of the two great Baroque giants, he was the more eclectic and universal, both in outlook, experience and appeal: and on him was bestowed the simplest yet most sublime tribute ever paid by one composer to another: 'Handel is the greatest composer that ever lived.' (Beethoven)

Chapter 1

Halle

On 23 April 1683, in St Bartholomew's Church, Giebichenstein (a suburb of the town of Halle, in Upper Saxony), Georg Händel, 61 years old and recently widowed, married the daughter of the aged Pastor of the parish. Dorothea Taust, then aged 32, had previously refused several offers of marriage in order to care for her infirm father after his wife's death, and those of her elder brother, her sister-in-law and her own young sister in a plague epidemic. However (as Dorothea's own funeral oration stated many years later), once her father had acquired a curate for his parish, enabling him to retire, 'this blessed woman was no longer able to resist the wise guidance of the Almighty, and the many persuasions of her father and other good friends, and resolved, after diligent prayer, in the name of God, to enter into Christian matrimony with him who had proposed to her, Herr Georg Händel, duly appointed Valet to H.R.H. August, Duke of Saxony, and *Administrator* Presumptive of the *Primate* Archbishopric of Magdeburg.'

Georg Händel took his bride to live at the House of the Golden Stag in the Kleine Klausstrasse (now the Grosse Nicolaistrasse) in Halle. His own family were middle-class, Protestant trades-people. On the death of his father Valentin, a coppersmith, Georg had been apprenticed to the trade of 'barber-surgeon', and, when his master died, Georg had taken over not only his business, but also – according to the custom of the time – his widow Anna, to whom he was married for some 40 years. During this time, Georg rose to become surgeon and *valet de chambre* to the local duke, August of Saxony; and on the duke's death in 1680, when Halle ceded its autonomy to the newly-emergent state of Prussia, he retained his post at the court of Duke Johann Adolf I at Weissenfels, about 30 kilometres to the south.

Founded in 961 on the Saale river, Halle, formerly the seat of the Margraves of Brandenburg, had been until the early seventeenth century a prosperous town in the heartland of orthodox

Lutheranism. Its musical tradition, too, was strongly Lutheran: in the early sixteenth century, Wolff Heintz, an organist much admired by Luther, had worked at the Liebfrauenkirche, one of the town's two principal churches; and a century later the composer Samuel Scheidt, up to then Halle's most celebrated musical son, had worked both as city organist and as *Kapellmeister* to the Margrave of Brandenburg. But the city suffered badly during the great European power struggle known as the Thirty Years War: from 1618 onwards, as rival Protestant and Catholic armies swept across the German states, ravaging the countryside and pillaging the towns, Halle – along with many other unfortunate communities in the battle zone – changed hands several times with ruinous consequences for its economy, losing almost half of its population in the process. Those who did survive had

Handel's father, Georg Händel.

14

HALL.

Moritzburg.

A view of Halle in the
seventeenth century.

to face recurrent outbreaks of plague: Scheidt lost all four of his children in the terrible epidemic of 1636. The arrival of the new administrator Duke August of Saxony in 1638 put an end to hostilities, but when the court removed to Weissenfels in 1680, Halle lost its former importance as a centre of patronage.

None-the-less, the Händel household enjoyed a comfortable standard of living. To the six children of Herr Händel's previous marriage, another four were added (the first, a boy, was stillborn in 1684). A year later, on 23 February 1685, Dorothea gave birth to her second and only surviving son, Georg Friedrich, who was baptised the next day at the Liebfrauenkirche; in due course he acquired two sisters, Dorothea Sophia and Johanna Christiana. All that is known of the composer's early childhood has survived only in Mainwaring's 1760 account, assembled from his conversations with Handel's amanuensis John Christopher Smith, who in turn had received his information from Handel himself. According to Mainwaring:

From his very childhood, HANDEL had discovered such a strong propensity to Music, that his father, who always intended him for the study of the Civil Law, had reason to be alarmed. Perceiving that this inclination still increased, he took every method to oppose it. He strictly forbade him to meddle with any musical instrument; nothing of that kind was suffered to remain in the house, nor was he ever permitted to go to any other, where such kind of furniture was in use. All this caution and art, instead of restraining, did but augment his passion. He had found means to get a little clavichord privately convey'd to a room at the top of the house. To this room he constantly stole when the family was asleep. He had made some progress before Music had been prohibited, and by his assiduous practice at the hours of rest, had made such farther advances, as, tho' not attended to at that time, were no slight prognostics of his future greatness.

15

This romantic determination to practise secretly during the night seems a little far-fetched: it is worth noting that some 30 years later, the English composer Thomas Arne (another budding composer intended by a strict father for the legal profession) claimed to have done exactly the same. However, by whatever means, the boy Handel quickly achieved a reasonable degree of fluency at the keyboard. Mainwaring relates how, at the age of six [now thought unlikely: the incident probably took place in 1696, when he was 11], Handel paid his first visit to his much-older half-brother Karl, *valet de chambre* to the Duke of Saxe-Weissenfels. His father, whose professional services were needed at court, wanted to leave the child at home, but young Handel was not so easily dissuaded. He followed his father's chaise on foot and, overtaking it some distance from the town, persuaded his unwilling parent to let him go with him.

Once at Weissenfels, Handel's father realised that he would never be able to keep an eye on his disobedient son, especially to 'keep him from getting at harpsichords'. He feared that if he gave way, the boy would soon lose all inclination for studying law – a far more lucrative and secure profession than music. Colleagues

The house where Handel was born in Halle.

and friends agreed in principle, but noting the lad's determination, 'some said, that, from all the accounts, the case appeared so desperate, that nothing but the cutting off of his fingers could prevent his playing; and others affirmed, that it was a pity any thing should prevent it.' Handel's father realised he was fighting a losing battle. According to Mainwaring:

it happened one morning, that while he was playing on the organ after the service was over, the Duke was in the church. Something there was in the manner of playing, which drew his attention so strongly, that his Highness, as soon as he returned, asked his *valet de chambre* who it was that he had heard at the organ, when the service was over. The valet replied, that it was his brother. The Duke demanded to see him.

After he had seen him, and made all the inquiries which it was natural for a man of taste and discernment to make on such an occasion, he told his physician, that every father must judge for himself in what manner to dispose of his children; but that, for his own part, he could not but consider it as a sort of crime against the public and prosperity, to rob the world of such a rising Genius!

An artist's impression of the boy Handel secretly practising the harpsichord in his parents' attic.

Handel's father argued that ' "though Music was an elegant

17

The Duke of Saxe-Weissenfels persuading Handel's father to allow his son to pursue a career in music. After a drawing by Woldemar Friedrich.

art, and a fine amusement, yet if considered as an occupation, it had little dignity, as having for its object nothing better than mere pleasure and entertainment: that whatever degree of eminence his son might arrive at in such a profession, he thought that a much less degree in many others would be far preferable." '

Eventually a compromise was reached. Handel would be allowed to study music in conjunction with his general education, and a music master was to be employed for the purpose. 'At his departure from Weisenfels [sic], the Prince fill'd his pockets with money, and told him, with a smile, that if he minded his studies, no encouragements should be wanting.'

The teacher selected was Friedrich Wilhelm Zachow (1663-1712), a native of Leipzig, who had been appointed organist and musical director of the Marienkirche in Halle in 1684. According to Mainwaring:

The Duke of Saxe-Weissenfels in his later years.

This person had great abilities in his profession, and was not more qualified than inclined to do justice to any pupil of a hopeful disposition. Handel pleased him so much, that he never thought he could do enough for him. The first object of his attention was to ground him thoroughly in the principles of harmony. His next care was to cultivate his imagination, and form his taste. He had a large collection of Italian as well as German music: he shewed him the different styles of different nations; the excellences and defects of each particular author; and, that he might equally advance in the practical part, he frequently gave him subjects to work, and made him copy, and play, and compose in his stead. Thus he had more exercise, and more experience than usually falls to the share of any learner at his years...

Among the composers whose works the young Handel is known to have studied are Froberger, Krieger (who had worked at Halle), Kerll, Alberti, Wolfgang Ebner, Strungk and Zachow himself. A manuscript apparently in Handel's hand, containing his copies of pieces by these and other German composers, survived until the late-eighteenth century. Handel apparently used it in turn to teach his own pupils.

According to Mainwaring, Handel continued to show no inclination to take up civil law, and soon became impatient with the limitations of Halle. In February 1697, the principal obstacle to the fulfilment of his ambitions was removed with his father's death, to which Handel responded with a conventionally anguished poem, beginning:

> Ah! heart's sorrow! my dearest father's heart
> Is wrenched from me by cruel death.
> Ah! bitter grief! Ah! what cruel anguish
> Seizes me, now that I am an orphan.

Nevertheless, his grief – though doubtless sincere – was tinged with a note of relief. Handel concluded defiantly:

Berlin viewed from the north, c. 1729.

Thus the early demise of his dearly beloved father, of blessed memory, is mourned by *Georg Friedrich Händel*, dedicated to the liberal arts.

Around the same time, according to Mainwaring, Handel
apparently visited Berlin. His prowess had brought him to the
notice of the Elector Friedrich III (later to become Friederich I,
King of Prussia) who 'frequently sent for him and made him large
presents', and offered to send him to Italy, all expenses paid, to
study under the best masters of the day. Handel's friends advised
caution: though the offer seemed a generous one, they feared that
it would place Handel under an intolerable obligation to the
Elector. 'For they well knew', continues Mainwaring, 'that if he
once engag'd in the King's [sic] service, he must remain in it,
whether he liked it, or not; that if he continued to please, it would
be a reason for not parting with him; and that if he happened to
displease, his ruin would be the certain consequence.' Handel's
father declined the offer on his son's behalf, pleading that he
himself had not long to live and wanted to keep his son near him.

In fact, Berlin in the late seventeenth century was not the
cultural and musical centre it later became under Frederick the
Great. From humble origins as a fishing village, Berlin had grown
in strategic and economic importance to become, by the mid-
fifteenth century, one of the principal cities of the Hanseatic
League. Just before the Thirty Years War, the electors of
Brandenburg had maintained there one of the largest court
orchestras of the time, numbering some 37 musicians; but the
establishment was subsequently decimated, and it was not until
Friedrich III became King of Prussia in 1701 that the Berlin court
once more became a centre of musical excellence. Friedrich
himself was not particularly interested in music: his own major
contribution to the promotion of the arts was the foundation in
1696 of the *Akademie der Künste*, which excluded music for more
than another century. The Electress Sophia Charlotte, however,
was an enthusiastic music-lover and amateur performer. As well
as taking part in chamber concerts, she had a small, private
theatre built in the Lietzenburg (now the Charlottenburg)
Palace, where she often accompanied opera performances on the
harpsichord, while encouraging her guests to take rôles on stage.
She was an ardent devotee of Italian music, and Mainwaring's
account of Handel's visit to Berlin relates how the boy was
introduced to two eminent Italian musicians temporarily
employed there, Giovanni Battista Bononcini and Attilio Ariosti,
both of whom Handel was to encounter again in later life.

Although Ariosti was working in Berlin in the latter part of
1697, Bononcini is known not to have arrived there until 1702,
which throws considerable doubt on Mainwaring's accuracy.
According to him, Bononcini, who was 'easily elated with
success, and apt to be intoxicated with admiration and applause',

Giovanni Battista Bononcini

resented the accolades given to young Handel, and resolved to put them to the test...

For this end he composed a Cantata in the chromatic style, difficult in every respect, and such as even a master, he thought, would be puzzled to play, or accompany without some previous practice. When he found that he, whom he had regarded as a mere child, treated this formidable composition as a mere trifle, not only executing it at sight, but with a degree of accuracy, truth, and expression hardly to be expected even from repeated practice; – then indeed he began to see him in another light, and to talk of him in another tone.

(Years later, Bononcini became one of Handel's greatest rivals in London, and relations between the two were always strained.) In contrast, Ariosti, who 'from the sweetness of his temper, and modesty of his character, was much more beloved as a man' (according to Mainwaring), 'would often take [Handel] on his knee, and make him play on his harpsichord for an hour together, equally pleased and surprized with the extraordinary proficiency of so young a person.' (If, as has been plausibly suggested, this visit actually dates from around 1703, then Handel must have been a strapping lad of 18. Either Ariosti had very strong knees, or the account is hopelessly confused!)

On 10 February 1702, Handel enrolled at Halle University. A month later, he was appointed organist at the Domkirche in place of one Johann Christoph Leporin, for whom he had apparently deputised in the past. For an honorarium of 50 thalers a year, plus free lodging, Handel undertook to 'play the organ fittingly at Divine Service' on Sundays, thanksgiving and feast days, to arrive at church 'always in good time and before the pealing of the bells ceases', to look after the organ itself, and to oversee any necessary repairs, 'to render to the Pastors and Elders set over him due honour and obedience, to live peaceably with the other Church Officers, and for the rest, to lead a Christian and edifying life.'

This peaceful and edifying existence failed to appeal for long to the ambitious 18-year-old. Mainwaring explains:

As his fortune was to depend on his skill in profession, it was necessary to consider of some place less distant [than Berlin] where he might employ his time to advantage, and be still improving in knowledge and experience. Next to the Opera of Berlin, that of HAMBURGH was in the highest request. It was resolved to send him thither on his own bottom, and chiefly with a view to improvement...

So in the summer of 1703, Handel set out for Hamburg.

Chapter 2

Hamburg

When that indefatigable traveller Dr Charles Burney visited Hamburg in 1772, he was agreeably surprised…

to find the entrance into this city free from examination, or custom-house embarrassments, the name only of a traveller being demanded at the gates. The streets are ill built, ill paved and narrow, but crowded with people who seem occupied with their own concerns; and there is an air of chearfulness, industry, plenty, and liberty, in the inhabitants of this place, seldom to be seen in other parts of Germany.

Unfettered by the restraints of court domination, the proud, mercantile city of Hamburg – the major trading centre of the northern part of Germany – cherished above all the freedom of its citizens. Responsibility for cultural activity lay with the municipal authorities, and music had flourished there since the mid-fourteenth century, with the formation of the first town band of salaried musicians. A century later, the eight or so municipal minstrels received official status as the *Ratsmusikanten*, at first under the direction of the council pastrycook, and then of the chief of police. By 1600, there were so many applications to join the civic band that the numbers were restricted to 15, and a retiring musician would sell his job to a younger successor, using the money received as a pension. From 1638 onwards, the council musicians sometimes took part in large-scale perform-ances of sacred music – central to Hamburg's strict Lutheran tradition. The most coveted musical post, which carried immense power and social prestige, was that of *Stadtkantor*, or *Musikdirektor der Hauptkirchen* – director of music for the city's five principal churches – who assumed overall responsibility for Hamburg's music, both sacred and secular. Thomas Selle, the influential *Stadtkantor* from 1637 to 1663, then established a core of ten professional singers, who joined the instrumentalists to provide the music for important civic functions, such as the

23

annual celebratory banquets of the citizen-captains, as well as taking part in the oratorio-Passions for which Hamburg was famous.

But during the second half of the seventeenth century, sacred music lost ground in Hamburg. The public wanted something more lively, and during Joachim Gerstenbüttel's tenure as *Stadtkantor* (1674-1721), the importance of his office declined. Taking advantage of official indifference, the municipal musicians tried to separate control of secular from sacred music by themselves assuming responsibility for the major civic festivals, thus marginalising the *Stadtkantor*'s importance. In 1678, the most important step towards secularisation occurred with the introduction of opera performances – in the teeth of bitter opposition from the church authorities, who regarded it as pernicious and immoral. Gerstenbüttel too opposed the opera, but his influence had waned and the new entertainment took root.

The first commercial opera company in Germany found a home in the newly-built *Oper-am-Gänsemarkt* (Goosemarket), an ugly Baroque building equipped with up-to-date machinery and a large stage. Its doors opened on 2 January 1678 with a drama on the subject of Adam and Eve, set to music by a local composer, Johann Theile. Since the staunchly Protestant burghers of Hamburg found it difficult to swallow the Italian concept of opera as a purely secular entertainment, sometimes based on myths and legends of dubious morality, Theile and his successors, Nicolaus Adam Strungk and Johann Wolfgang Francke, kept the house open for its first 12 years or so by staging a series of dull but safe operas based mainly on biblical texts, intermixed with mythological or historical subject matter and leavened with a dash of comedy. Even so, their productions were closely scrutinised for any hint of licentiousness by the censorious 'church police'.

By the early 1690s, the French operatic style evolved over the past two decades by Jean-Baptiste Lully (court composer to Louis XIV and founder of the *Académie royale de musique* in Paris), had been introduced to Hamburg by two successive

Hamburg in the seventeenth century.

24

directors of the *Gänsemarkt*, Johann Georg Conradi and Johann Sigismund Kusser. Kusser had studied in Paris with Lully, and the few airs that survive from his five Hamburg operas show the prevailing influence of French style. Taking his cue from the autocratic Lully, whose orchestral discipline was famed throughout Europe, Kusser set out to raise the standard of playing at the *Gänsemarkt*; but – restless by nature – he moved on after just over a year. With a series of over 50 operas, written over a period of two decades in a synthesis of the Italian and French styles, and characterised by a real sense of theatre allied to inventive orchestration, Kusser's brilliant young successor Reinhard Keiser consolidated Hamburg's position as one of the major northern European operatic centres. It was Keiser's reputation that drew Handel to Hamburg in 1703.

According to Mainwaring, Handel's first move was to find some pupils and a job playing in the opera orchestra. 'Such was his industry and success in setting out, that the first remittance which his mother sent him he generously returned her, accompanied with a small present of his own.' On 9 July, in the organ loft of the Church of St Mary Magdalene, Handel met a young man of much his own age named Johann Mattheson. The son of a socially ambitious tax-collector, the prodigiously talented Mattheson had studied dancing, drawing, riding, fencing and languages, in addition to his formal education. Under the tuition of *Stadtkantor* Gerstenbüttel, he had learnt to play the flute, oboe, lute, gamba and violin; while his singing voice, even as a child, had attracted the attention of the opera house director, who invited him to join the company. Although originally destined (like Handel) for a career in law, Mattheson enjoyed his work at the opera house so much that he forfeited a university place to stay on. He first appeared as a soloist in 1696, thereafter singing many tenor rôles – not always with total success – and conducting rehearsals. In 1699, his first opera, *Die Plejades*, was performed by the company.

Mattheson went on to become the most important German theorist of his age. His voluminous legacy includes *Der volkommene Capellmeister* (1739), a compendium of information for the training of a *Kapellmeister*, or musical director; and the *Grundläge einer Ehren-Pforte* (1740), an invaluable biographical lexicon of nearly 150 musicians, past and present – information on the latter being derived from Mattheson's own correspondence and conversations with the musicians themselves. He also left a biographical sketch of Handel, which includes an account of their relationship:

Handel came to Hamburg in the summer of 1703, rich in ability and

goodwill. I was almost the first with whom he became acquainted, and through me he was introduced to all the choirs and organs, operas and concerts here, especially a particular house where music reigned supreme. At first he played *ripieno* violin in the opera orchestra, and behaved as if he knew nothing, having a naturally dry sense of humour... But once when the harpsichord player failed to appear he allowed himself to be persuaded to take his place, and acquitted himself manfully – something only I had previously suspected. At that time he composed very lengthy airs, and almost interminable cantatas, which had neither the right kind of skill nor taste, though proficient in harmony, but the lofty schooling of opera soon knocked him into shape... He was a skilful organist, better than Kuhnau in fugue and counterpoint, especially *ex tempore*, but he knew very little about melodic writing until he came to the Hamburg opera.

Mattheson and Handel quickly became close friends. Less than a week after their first meeting, they took a river excursion; at the end of the month they played the organ together in the Church of St Mary Magdalene, with a pastry-cook's son pumping the bellows; and in mid-August they both set off by post-chaise for Lübeck, where Dietrich Buxtehude – then nearing retirement age – was organist of St Mary's. Mattheson takes up the story:

On 17 August, we journeyed to Lübeck, and in the carriage made many double fugues *de mente, non da penna*. I had been invited by Magnus von Wedderkopp, the president of the council, to compete for the post of successor to the renowned organist Dietrich Buxtehude, and I took Handel with me. We played on almost all the organs and harpsichords in the place, and made an agreement... that he should only play the organ and I only the harpsichord. However, it turned out that there was a marriage condition attached to the appointment, for which we neither of us felt the slightest desire, so we said goodbye to the place, after having enjoyed ourselves extremely and received many gratifying tokens of respect.

The 'marriage condition' – in this case the hand of Buxtehude's ageing and unattractive daughter – also proved a sticking point two years later, when J.S. Bach applied for the job. Eventually, one Johann Christian Schiefferdecker bit the bullet and succeeded Buxtehude in 1707.

Mattheson's social connections also found Handel a teaching job – as harpsichord tutor to Cyril Wyche, son of the English Ambassador to Hamburg. But towards the end of 1704, the two friends quarrelled violently, resulting in a duel which almost cost Handel his life. Mattheson relates:

On 5 December, when my third opera, *Cleopatra*, was being performed with Handel at the harpsichord, a misunderstanding arose: such a thing is nothing new with ambitious and inconsiderate young people. I, as composer, directed, and at the same time sang the part of Antonius, who, about half-an-hour before the end of the play, commits suicide. Now until that occasion I had been accustomed thereafter to go into the orchestra and accompany the rest myself, which unquestionably the composer can do better than anyone else; this time, however, Handel refused to surrender his place. Incited by several people, we fought a duel at the exit of the Opera House, in the public market place and before a crowd of onlookers. Things might have passed off very unfortunately for both of us, had not God's guidance graciously ordained that my blade, thrusting against the broad, metal coat-button of my opponent, should be shattered. No real harm came of the affair, and through the intervention of one of the most eminent councillors in Hamburg, we were soon reconciled again; and I had the honour, on the same day, 30 December, of entertaining Handel to dinner after which

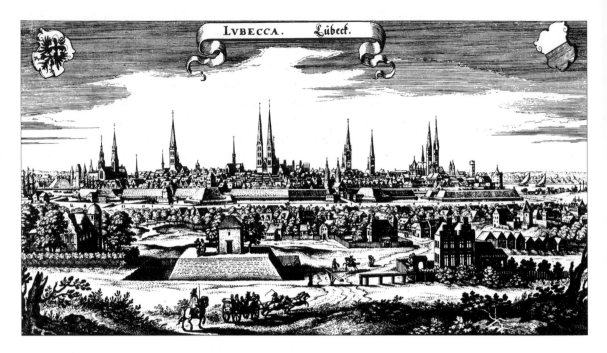

A view of Lübeck

we went in the evening to the rehearsal of his *Almira*, and became better friends than before.

When Mainwaring related this incident, he embroidered it – much to Mattheson's disgust – into an attempted murder rather than a duel, with Mattheson attacking the unarmed Handel as he came out of the orchestra, death being prevented by a 'friendly Score', which Handel was hugging to his chest. However, Mattheson's assertion that the incident did nothing to damage his friendship with Handel may also have been wishful thinking. Later in life, despite frequent and increasingly intemperate pestering by Mattheson, Handel resolutely declined to supply any autobiographical material for Mattheson's great lexicon.

By now, Handel was already composing: a number of keyboard suites are thought to date from this period, while Mainwaring mentions 'a considerable number of sonatas' which Handel was 'so imprudent as to let [go] out of his hands', and are lost. Other works thought to date from Handel's Hamburg years, including two Passion settings, are now known to be spurious. *Almira*, however, was his first major composition, and his first attempt at opera – a genre which would henceforth be central to his life and works.

According to Mainwaring, Handel wrote *Almira* to fill a gap during one of Reinhard Keiser's periodic absences due to financial embarrassment. This may not be true: in 1704, Keiser and his partner, the text adaptor Drusicke, were running the theatre, which certainly underwent an enforced closure for a period that year. But Keiser was enormously prolific: during the four years of his directorship (1703-1707), he wrote some 17 operas, and it seems unlikely that none was available for production. It is more probable that Keiser invited Handel, along with Mattheson and another composer, to contribute to the repertory. According to some sources, he may have regretted his decision, since shortly afterwards he himself reset Handel's chosen texts, perhaps to emphasise his own superiority as a composer.

Hoping to appeal to local taste, Handel's librettist Friedrich Christian Feustking adapted a former Italian libretto into an unwieldy macaronic mixture of Italian and German, with French-style ballet sequences. The story gave Handel the opportunity to show his paces in some spectacular set pieces, including a coronation scene and a masque for the continents. One instrumental piece, a saraband called *Danse des Asiates*, served Handel well in later years when it reappeared as the aria 'Lascia ch'io pianga' in *Rinaldo*.

With Mattheson as principal tenor, *Almira* opened on 8 January 1705 and ran for 20 nights. The music appears to have been well-received, but Feustking's libretto evidently attracted criticism, since he felt obliged to reply publicly to 'malicious unreasonableness or unreasonable malice'. The main thrust of the attack, perhaps motivated by jealousy, may have come from Keiser's librettist Barthold Feind, who shortly afterwards prepared a version of the same text for Keiser.

Encouraged by the success of *Almira*, Handel rapidly wrote a second opera, based on the life of the bloodthirsty Roman emperor Nero (the full title is *Die durch Blut und Mord erlangete Liebe, oder, Nero* – Love obtained by Blood and Murder, or, Nero). Premièred on 25 February 1705, just six weeks after *Almira*, it was a flop, and was taken off after just three performances. Once again a lifeless libretto was harshly criticised, criticism with which Handel is supposed to have concurred. The score, which apparently contained a high proportion of ballet scenes, is lost.

Handel's third and last opera for Hamburg was begun in 1706, but did not reach the stage until early 1708, by which time he had left for Italy, and Keiser – beset by debts – had handed over the lease of the theatre to another impresario. The music for *Florindo* (based on the Greek myth of Daphne, betrothed to Florindo but loved by Phoebus, and finally rescued from an impossible situation by transformation into a laurel-tree), proved so long-winded that the opera had to be divided into two parts, *Happy Florindo* and *Transformed Daphne*, in order not to 'put the audience out of humour'. Again, the score is lost, but it is likely that Handel re-used some of the material in later works.

By 1706, the financial and artistic situation at the Hamburg Opera was becoming increasingly precarious. According to Mainwaring, the new manager of the opera house offered Handel a permanent post as composer to the opera, which he declined on the grounds that 'he came thither only as a traveller, and with a view to improvement: that till the Composer should be at liberty, or till some other successor or substitute could be found, he was willing to be employed, but was resolved to see more of the world before he entered into any engagements which would confine him long to any particular place.' Mainwaring continues:

At the time that ALMERIA [sic] and FLORINDA were performed, there were many persons of note at Hamburgh, among whom was the Prince of Tuscany [Prince Ferdinando], brother to John Gaston de Medicis, Grand Duke. The Prince was a great lover of the art for which his country is so renowned. Handel's proficiency in it, not only procured him access to his Highness, but occasioned a sort of intimacy betwixt them: they frequently discoursed together on the state of Music in general, and on the merits of Composers, Singers, and Performers in particular. The Prince would often lament that Handel was not acquainted with those of Italy; shewed him a large collection of Italian Music; and was very desirous he should return with him to Florence. Handel plainly confessed that he could see nothing in the Music which answered the high character his Highness had given it. On the contrary, he thought it so very indifferent, that the Singers, he said, must be angels to recommend it. The Prince smiled at the severity of his censure, and added, that there needed nothing but a journey to Italy to reconcile him to the style and taste which prevailed there... The Prince then intimated, that if he chose to return with him, no conveniences should be wanting. Handel, without intending to accept of the favour designed him, expressed his sense of the honour done him. For he resolved to go to Italy on his own bottom, as soon as he could make a purse for that occasion. This noble spirit of independency, which possessed him almost from his childhood, was never known to forsake him, not even in the most distressful seasons of his life.

Apart from the regular allowances which Handel had continued to make to his mother, he had, according to Mainwaring, saved up 'a purse of 200 ducats. On the strength of this fund he resolved to set out for Italy.'

Chapter 3

Italy

A man who has not been in Italy is always conscious of an inferiority, from his not having seen what it is expected a man should see. The grand object of travelling is to see the shores of the Mediterranean. (Dr Johnson)

In the autumn of 1706, the 21-year-old Handel arrived in Florence, the city of Dante, Petrarch and Boccaccio, and the birthplace of opera. 'Florence, the chief City of Tuscany, Seat of an Archbishop, and Residence of the Great Duke, is situated on the River Arno, as it were in the middle of the Arena or bottom of an Amphitheater. At the distance of four or five miles...it is surrounded with very fertile Hillocks, which rise insensibly, and by degrees unite themselves to the high Mountains. The vast number of Houses which cover both the little Hills, and the

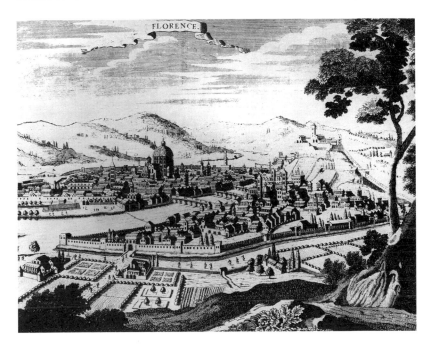

Florence, c. 1720.

Bronze statue by Donatello; *David with the head of Goliath* c. 1430.

interjacent Plain, make a very delightful and admirable Prospect... it may be justly said, that this rich and delicious Valley is the best inhabited place in the World', wrote the French traveller Maximilian Misson in the early 1690s.

For nearly three hundred years, the wealthy and politically astute Medici family had ruled Florence, establishing a court unrivalled for its cultural splendour. Under their patronage, jewels of Renaissance architecture such as Michelozzi's Medici Palace and the serene but austere family church of San Lorenzo, built by the architectural genius Brunelleschi, had augmented Florence's unrivalled collection of Gothic and Romanesque buildings; while the sculptural masterpieces of Donatello, Verrochio, Ghiberti, Michelangelo and Cellini and the art treasures of Masaccio, Gozzoli, Fra Angelico, Lippi, Uccello and

Donatello school; *Madonna and child with angels*, S. Croce, Florence.

32

Michelangelo; detail from the grave of Lorenzo de' Medici, church of San Lorenzo, Florence. c. 1524-27.

Ghirlandaio richly endowed the city's squares, churches and private palaces.

Having acquired the services of the greatest artists of the time, the Medici also employed some of the finest European musicians.

In the mid-sixteenth century, Duke Cosimo I, employer of Marenzio, Caccini, Peri, Cavalieri, and Antonio and Vittoria Archilei, initiated the practice of celebrating the milestones of family life and the arrival of distinguished guests with magnificent entertainments involving feasting, dancing and plays with musical interludes, known as *intermedi*. From these spectacular productions evolved the earliest operas, such as Peri's *Euridice*, performed in the great theatre of the Pitti Palace to celebrate the historic union of Maria de'Medici and Henri IV of France in 1600.

When Handel arrived just over a century later, the Medici dynasty was nearing its end. Grand Duke Cosimo III (reigned 1670-1723) was not particularly fond of music; but his son, the heir apparent, Prince Ferdinando (1663-1713), loved it passionately. A fine executant (he is said to have been able to play a difficult piece at sight on the harpsichord, and then repeat it from memory), Ferdinando encouraged both the practice and the creation of music. Private chamber concerts were held almost every evening in his apartments; twice a year, during Carnival and in the autumn, he directed opera performances at his private theatre, and, following the lead of his ancestors, he surrounded himself with the finest musicians of the day, including Pasquini, Veracini, and Alessandro and Domenico Scarlatti. The Prince was a true 'Renaissance' man: he was skilled not only in music, but also in art, literature and science. In his private workshop, he helped Bartolomeo Cristofori to invent the pianoforte. Sadly, his premature death marked the end of Medici patronage of the arts: his brother Gian Gastone, who succeeded to the title in 1723 and died without an heir 14 years later, showed no interest in cultural activities.

Having invited Handel to Florence, Ferdinando was impatient to try out his new protégé. Mainwaring outlines the situation:

The fame of his [Handel's] abilities had raised the curiosity of the Duke [Cosimo III] and his court, and rendered them very impatient to have some performance of his composing. With less experience, and fewer years to mature his judgment, he had hitherto succeeded to the utmost extent of his wishes. But he was now to be brought to trial in a strange country, where the style was as different from that of his own nation, as the manners and customs of the Italians are from those of the Germans. Sensible as he was of this disadvantage, his ambition would not suffer him to decline the trial to which he was invited.

Ferdinando II de' Medici. 1610-1670. Grand Duke of Tuscany.

Handel resolved to beat the Italians at their own game. In November 1707, his three-act opera *Rodrigo* – or, to give it its full title *Vincer se stesso è la maggior vittoria* (To Conquer Oneself is the Greater Victory) – was performed at a theatre in the Via di Cocomero, under the patronage of Prince Ferdinando. The opera – whose historical plot concerns the rape of the noblewoman Florinda by Rodrigo, last of the Spanish Visigothic kings, setting in motion a chain of disastrous consequences culminating in the Moorish invasion of Spain – was well-received: Handel was officially rewarded with a gift of 100 sequins and a dinner service. A less tangible – and politically dubious – reward was also offered. The soprano title rôle in *Rodrigo* was apparently designed for Grand Duke Cosimo's mistress, the famous singer Vittoria Tarquini (known as *'La Bombace'*), who for some unknown reason did not take part in the opera. However, according to Mainwaring, Tarquini was 'so little sensible of her exalted situation' that she 'conceived a design of transferring her affections to another person. Handel's youth and comeliness, joined with his fame and abilities in Music, had made impressions on her heart'. Although it seems unlikely that Handel would have openly risked incurring the wrath of the Grand Duke by stealing his mistress, he certainly acquired the reputation of having been her lover.

Between his first arrival in Florence and the performance of *Rodrigo*, Handel went to Rome. There, in contrast to the Renaissance grace of Florence, the ancient ruins of a vanished empire vied with the flamboyant, swirling Baroque extravaganzas of Bernini. ''Tis impossible to walk fifty paces in or about that City without observing some Remainders of its ancient Grandeur', observed Misson. 'This proud City was adorn'd with Temples, Palaces, Theatres...Triumphal Arches, Baths, Cirques, Columns, Fountains, Aqueducts, Obelisks, Mausoleums, and other Magnificent Structures; but now all these Things may be truly said to be buried in their own Ruins, tho' these Ruins, as dismal as they are, seem still to retain a great deal of their ancient splendor.'

Unlike the temporal magnificence of the Medici court, political and cultural activity in Rome was dominated by spiritual authority. Since the fifteenth century, successive popes had enlarged and strengthened their musical establishments, both at the Sistine Chapel within the walls of the Vatican palace, and at St Peter's Church. Palestrina, the first official *maestro di cappella* at the Vatican, was succeeded by an illustrious line of musicians and organists; and other Roman churches, including St John Lateran and St Maria Maggiore, followed the papal example.

Rome, c. 1729.

35

Nor was entertainment of a more secular nature lacking in Rome. Although public access to opera was limited (the first public opera house, the Teatro Tordinona, had a chequered career, alternately open, closed or demolished according to the moral stance of the current occupant of the Vatican), the luxurious private palaces of Rome's epicurean cardinals, as well as the residences of exiled monarchs such as Queen Christina of Sweden, offered unlimited opportunity for a variety of sensual delights. Among these, music featured prominently.

In 1632, Cardinals Antonio and Francesco Barberini had set a precedent by building a private theatre seating 3,000 in the Barberini Palace; their example was later followed by two more opera-lovers and enthusiastic amateur librettists, Cardinals Benedetto Pamphili and Pietro Ottoboni. During the summer months, when the cardinals retired to their sumptuous villas which dotted the surrounding hills, guests would assemble on flower-bedecked terraces in the cool of the evening to hear float-loads of singers and instrumentalists performing *al fresco* cantatas and serenades. Although female singers were officially frowned upon by the church authorities (Pope Sixtus V had issued a decree banning women from appearing on stage), no one could legislate against private performances; and, in any

Photo taken in 1890 of the Barberini Palace, Rome.

case, the problem could be circumvented by using male sopranos. (Such singers, castrated in childhood to preserve the purity of their unbroken voices, were highly prized and well-paid for their sacrifice: during the eighteenth century they were the mainstay of Italian *opera seria* all over Europe.)

'A German has arrived in this city who is an excellent player of the harpsichord and composer. Today he exhibited his abilities by playing the organ in the church of St John [Lateran] to general admiration', noted a Roman diarist on 14 January 1707. Mainwaring explains further:

The fame of [Handel's] musical achievements... had reached that metropolis long before him. His arrival therefore was immediately known, and occasioned civil enquiries and polite messages from persons of the first distinction there. Among his greatest admirers was the Cardinal Ottoboni, a person of a refined taste, and princely magnificence. Besides a fine collection of pictures and statues, he had a large library of Music, and an excellent band of performers, which he kept in constant pay.

Pietro Ottoboni (1667-1740), vice-chancellor of the Catholic Church, was one of the richest, most influential and most profligate of all the Roman cardinals. But even his vast wealth could hardly cope with the lavish performances mounted at his residence, the Palazzo della Cancelleria. According to a French diplomat, 'His Eminence employs the best musicians and performers in Rome, and amongst others the famous Arcangelo Corelli and young Paolucci, who is considered the finest voice in Europe, so that every Wednesday he has an excellent concert in his palace.' In addition, 'it was a customary thing with his eminence to have performances of Operas, Oratorios, and such other grand compositions, as could from time to time be procured', continues Mainwaring. 'Handel was desired to furnish his quota; and there was always such a greatness and superiority in the pieces composed by him, as rendered those of the best masters comparatively little and insignificant.'

One of Handel's first Roman compositions was the serenata *Il trionfo del Tempo e del Disinganno* (The Triumph of Time and Truth), which was performed in the late spring of 1707. The librettist was Ottoboni's great rival, Cardinal Pamphili; but since Corelli, the finest violinist in Europe – who was employed by Ottoboni from 1690 to 1713 – led the orchestra, it seems likely that the performance took place at one of Ottoboni's *accademie*. According to Mainwaring:

[Corelli] complained of the difficulty he found in playing [Handel's] Overtures. Indeed there was in the whole cast of these compositions,

Arcangelo Corelli, violinist and composer.

but especially in the opening of them, such a degree of fire and force, as never could consort with the mild graces, and placid elegancies of a genius so totally dissimilar. Several fruitless attempts Handel had one day made to instruct him in the manner of executing these spirited passages. Piqued at the tameness with which he still played them, he snatched the instrument out of his hand; and, to convince him how little he understood them, played the passages himself. But CORELLI, who was a person of great modesty and meekness, wanted no conviction of this sort; for he ingenuously declared that he did not understand them; i.e. knew not how to execute them properly, and give them the strength and expression they required. When Handel appeared impatient, "Ma, caro Sassone" (said he), "questa Musica é nel stylo Francese, di ch'io non m'intendo." [But, my dear German, this music is in the French style, which I don't understand.]

Mainwaring also states that Corelli had the greatest difficulty with the overture to *Il trionfo del Tempo*, persuading Handel to replace it with 'a symphony... more in the Italian style'.

Among the musicians whom Handel encountered at the Palazzo della Cancelleria were the Scarlattis, father and son. Although Domenico Scarlatti, the third of the great Baroque trio born in 1685, had not yet begun to compose the harpsichord music which later made his name, he was already rated as one of the best keyboard performers of the day. According to Mainwaring, Cardinal Ottoboni arranged a contest of skill between him and Handel. Scarlatti was apparently judged the better harpsichordist, but when it came to the organ, 'there was not the least pretence for doubting to which of them [the preference] belonged. SCARLATTI himself declared the superiority of his antagonist, and owned ingenuously that till he had heard him upon this instrument, he had no conception of its powers... Though no two persons ever arrived at such perfection on their respective instruments', continues Mainwaring, 'yet it is remarkable that there was a total difference in their manner. The characteristic excellence of SCARLATTI seems to have consisted in a certain elegance and delicacy of expression. Handel had an uncommon brilliancy and command of finger: but what distinguished him from all other players who possessed these same qualities, was that amazing fulness, force and energy, which he joined with them.'

Mainwaring also relates that Handel's spiritual patrons duly attempted to reform his Lutheran ways, and 'lead him out of the road to damnation'. Handel stubbornly replied that he was 'resolved to die a member of that communion, whether true or false, in which he was born and bred', and the cardinals soon realised that he was a man of 'honest, though mistaken principles, and therefore concluded that he would not easily be induced to change them.' Nevertheless, he was prepared to compromise his Protestant principles sufficiently to provide music for the annual Vesper service for the feast-day of the Madonna del Carmine, celebrated on 16 July in the church of S Maria di Monte Santo in the Piazza del Popolo. The music, performed with no expense spared, was commissioned by another Roman cardinal, Carlo Colonna, who had connections with the Carmelite order. Handel had apparently already completed two sections, the psalm *Dixit Dominus* and the antiphon *Salve regina;* to these he now added two more psalms, *Laudate pueri* and *Nisi Dominus,* and three antiphons: *Te decus virginem* (believed lost, and only rediscovered in 1984), *Haec est regina virginem* and *Saeviat tellus.* Handel's vivid, extrovert settings show an immediate and sympathetic response both to the unfamiliar Catholic liturgy, and to the current Italian sacred style.

Between May and October 1707, Handel found employment in the household of the Marquis Francesco Maria di Ruspoli. One of the richest laymen in Rome, Ruspoli employed around 80 people, including cooks, huntsmen and a small number of virtuoso musical performers – among them the celebrated soprano Margherita Durastante, the cellist Filippo Amadei, and the father and son Domenico and Pietro Castrucci (both violinists) – at his

View of the Piazza del Popolo, where Handel's music for the Vesper service was performed.

39

Roman residence, the Palazzo Bonelli in the Piazza SS Apostoli, and in his country mansions at Vignanello and Cerveteri. Handel returned to Ruspoli's employment for two further periods, in the spring and autumn of 1708. His contract was flexible: although he received no regular salary, he was expected to supply secular cantatas for Sunday performance, for which he was presumably 'rewarded'. The cream of Roman society attended these *accademie,* which were intended to evoke a vanished pastoral Arcadia. Members gave themselves fictional Ancient Greek shepherds' names, recited poetry in the 'classical' style, and listened to appropriately pastoral music. The position of 'host' of the Accademia degli Arcadia changed annually: in 1708, it was the turn of the Marquis Ruspoli. His *accademie,* said to be the best in Rome, included performances of cantatas with *continuo* accompaniment only (given by the household musicians), and more elaborate works with full instrumental accompaniment, for which freelance players were brought in. Altogether, Handel supplied some 40 cantatas in the first category, including *Lucretia,* and eight or so with more elaborate instrumentation: these included *Armida abbandonata* and *Diana cacciatrice.* One of the *continuo* cantatas, *Hendel, non può mia Musa,* set a text by Cardinal Pamphili comparing Handel to Orpheus (a comparison later elaborated at length by different eulogists), and extolling his ability to rouse the librettist's torpid Muse once more.

In the autumn of 1707, Handel returned to Florence for the production of *Rodrigo.* By February 1708, he was back in Rome, where, since a papal ban on opera was still in force, his patron Ruspoli commissioned from him the next best thing – a sacred drama on the subject of the Resurrection, which was to be staged with no expense spared on Easter Sunday. For the production of *La resurrezione* – Handel's first oratorio – a special stage was constructed in the main hall on the ground floor of the Marquis's palace, with four rows of terraced seats to accommodate a large orchestra. At the front, the orchestral leader (Corelli), his second violin, and Handel at the harpsichord sat together on a special raised platform; while the musicians played from 28 special music-stands in gold *chiaroscuro*, half painted with the Marquis's coat-of-arms, and half with his wife's. Above the proscenium was hung a cartoon depicting cherubs, palm-trees and foliage, with the title of the oratorio picked out in back-lit translucent paper in the centre. The stage, lit by 16 candelabras, was hidden by an ornate taffeta curtain, which rose to reveal an elaborate canvas back-drop, featuring the Resurrection as its centrepiece. The hall was swathed in red and yellow taffeta, and in crimson velvet trimmed with gold. Ruspoli engaged an orchestra of at least 45 players, including 23 violins. Corelli himself received almost four times the usual orchestral rate for the occasion – but Handel, who is not known to have been paid in cash, may have received other rewards. The expenses for the occasion list payments for five rings, set with diamonds and other gems; while a large food-bill paid by Ruspoli's Master of the Household for 'Monsù Endel and company' indicates that at least he was well-fed!

No account of the actual performance survives: it earned a laconic mention in a diary of the period: 'This evening the Marchese Ruspoli had a very fine musical oratorio performed in the Bonelli palace at the SS Apostoli, having set up in the great hall a magnificent theatre for the audience. Many of the nobility and a few cardinals were present.' The following day, the Marquis was reprimanded personally by the Pope, for allowing a female singer (Margherita Durastante, who took the part of Mary Magdalene) to perform in the oratorio.

From May 1708, Handel spent about ten weeks in Naples – an obligatory stop on the eighteenth-century Grand Tour – where, according to Mainwaring, he 'had a palazzo at command, and was provided with table, coach, and all other accommodations... While he was at Naples he received invitations from most of the principal persons who lived within reach of that capital; and lucky was he esteemed, who could engage him soonest, and detain him longest...' It is not known whether he found time to visit the famous local antiquities which so delighted Dr Burney; but

Copper engraving of Venice, 1693, after P. Coronelli.

during his stay he wrote a one-act pastoral serenata, *Aci, Galatea, e Polifemo*, which was performed at the wedding of the Duke of Alvito to Donna Beatrice Sanseverino on 19 July 1708. Ten years later, Handel used the same story – the tragic love of Acis and Galatea, destroyed by the jealousy of the giant Polyphemus – for his English masque *Acis and Galatea*, but the two settings are musically entirely different.

Handel spent the winter of 1708-1709 in Rome with Ruspoli. But according to Mainwaring, 'the nature of his design in travelling made it improper for him to stay long in any one place... It was his resolution to visit every part of Italy, which was in any way famous for its musical performances. Venice was his next resort...'

By the second half of the seventeenth century, Venice, once the trading, if not the cultural, centre of Europe, was already in political, economic and artistic decline. Monteverdi's death in 1643 had marked the end of the golden age of Venetian sacred music; and during the second half of the seventeenth century, the increasing secularisation of public life had aroused renewed interest in opera. The first Venetian opera house, S Cassiano, had opened in 1637; and by the time Handel visited the city, opera was offered for three periods a year – Carnival, Ascensiontide and the autumn – in at least six public theatres, built and owned by noble families, but run by impresarios. Lacking the enormous wealth of the Roman cardinals, the prime concern of Venetian merchant-princes was value for money; so opera producers and designers became adept at achieving effective results on a limited budget. Furthermore, Venetian audiences were not limited to aristocratic circles. Anyone – whether a citizen of the Republic or a visiting foreigner – was free to attend, for the price of a seat (two lire).

Venice invented the carnival, an idea quickly imitated by every other Italian city. From Christmas until the beginning of Lent, the city devoted itself to the unremitting pursuit of pleasure, from opera to street theatre, from private balls to spectacular public displays. Aristocratic palaces, piazzas and canals alike were the scene of the famous masquerades, during which elaborate costumes and masks provided cover for many a discreet liaison. Misson took a censorious view of Venice in carnival time:

The Carnival always begins the second Holiday in Christmas; that is to say, from thence they are permitted to wear Masks, and to open the Play-Houses and Gaming-Houses: Then they are not satisfied with the ordinary Libertinism, they improve all their Pleasures, and plunge into them up to the neck. All the City is disguis'd; Vice and Vertue were never so well counterfeited... Strangers and Courtesans come in shoals from all parts of Europe. There is every where a general Motion and Confusion. You would swear, that all the World were turn'd Fools in an Instant... The greatest Masquerading is in the place of St Mark; where the Crowd is sometimes so great, that one cannot turn himself... The Women are Habited as they please, and are to be seen there in most magnificent Dresses. In the mean time the place is filled with Puppet-Plays, Rope-Dancers and all sorts of such People as you see at *Bartholomew-Fair...*

It was at one of these masquerades that Handel met up again with Domenico Scarlatti. According to Mainwaring:

[Handel] was first discovered there at a Masquerade, while he was playing on a harpsichord in his visor. SCARLATTI happened to be there, and affirmed it could be no one but the famous Saxon, or the devil. Being thus detected, he was strongly importuned to compose an Opera. But there was so little prospect of either honour or advantage from such an undertaking, that he was very unwilling to engage in it...

Masked Venetians, painting by Pietro Longhi (1702-85).

43

According to Joseph Addison, a famous English journalist:

Opera's are another great Entertainment of this [Carnival] Season. The Poetry of 'em is generally so exquisitely ill, as the Musick is good. The Arguments are often taken from some celebrated Action of the ancient Greeks and Romans, which sometimes looks ridiculous enough, for who can endure to hear one of the rough old Romans squeaking thro' the Mouth of an Eunuch...

Lacking Addison's English squeamishness, Handel no doubt enjoyed hearing works by leading Italian composers, including Alessandro Scarlatti and Antonio Caldara. He then returned to Florence for most of 1709, but by Christmas, he was back in Venice. There, at the beginning of the Carnival season, his own opera *Agrippina*, to a libretto by the Viceroy of Naples, Cardinal Vincenzo Grimani, was produced at the Grimani family theatre, S Giovanni Crisostomo. Its distinguished cast included Durastanti in the title rôle, the bass Antonio Francesco Carli as Claudio, and the castrato Valeriano Pellegrini as Nero. Mainwaring relates:

In three weeks he finished his AGRIPPINA, which was performed twenty-seven nights successively; and in a theatre which had been shut up for a long time, notwithstanding there were two other Opera-houses open at the same time; at one of which GASPARINI presided, as LOTTI did at the other. The audience was so enchanted with this performance, that a stranger who should have seen the manner in which they were affected, would have imagined they had all been distracted.

The theatre, at almost every pause, resounded with shouts of acclamations of *'viva il caro Sassone!'* and other expressions of approbation too extravagant to be mentioned. They were thunderstruck with the grandeur and sublimity of his stile: for never had they known till then all the powers of harmony and modulation so closely arrayed, and so forcibly combined.

Agrippina, a melodrama of intrigue woven with scant regard for historical accuracy around the figures of the Roman Emperor Claudius, his wife Agrippina, and the future emperor Nero, represented the peak of Handel's achievement during his three years in Italy. He had come into contact with the finest Italian musicians of the time, particularly Alessandro Scarlatti, from whom he had absorbed the technique of writing for the voice in fluid, seamless melodies; while his instrumental style had been refined by his collaboration with Corelli. In the words of the Handel scholar Winton Dean, writing in *The New Grove,* 'he arrived in Italy a gifted but crude composer with an uncertain command of form, and left it a polished and fully equipped artist'.

'Handel having now been long enough in Italy effectually to

answer the purpose of his going thither, began to think of returning to his native country. Not that he intended this to be the end of his travels; for his curiosity was not yet allay'd, nor likely to be so while there was any musical court which he had not yet seen.'(Mainwaring). During his visit to Venice, Handel had been introduced to Prince Ernst of Hanover, younger brother of the Elector, Georg Ludwig. The Prince and his Master of Horse, Baron Kielmansegge, pressed the young composer, now nearly 25, to visit Hanover. At the same time, Handel had received other invitations: one from Prince Carl von Neuburg, Governor of the Tyrol; and another from the English Ambassador to Venice, the Duke of Manchester, who suggested that he should go to London. Bearing all these in mind, and no doubt homesick after his three-year absence, Handel left Italy in February 1710. After a brief stop in Innsbruck, where he declined the Prince von Neuburg's offer of a job, he went on to Hanover. According to Mainwaring:

At Hanover there was also a Nobleman who had taken great notice of Handel in Italy, and who did him great service (as will appear soon) when he came to ENGLAND for the second time. This person was Baron KILMANSECK [sic]. He introduced him at court, and so well recommended him to his Electoral Highness, that he immediately offered him a pension of 1500 Crowns per annum as an inducement to

Hanover, c. 1700.

stay. Tho' such an offer from a Prince of his character was not to be neglected, Handel loved liberty too well to accept it hastily, and without reserve. He told the Baron how much he owed to his kind and effectual recommendation, as well as to his Highness's goodness and generosity. But he also expressed his apprehensions that the favour intended him would hardly be consistent either with the promise he had actually made to visit the court of the Elector Palatine, or with the resolution he had long taken to pass over into England, for the sake of seeing that of LONDON. Upon this objection, the Baron consulted his Highness's pleasure, and Handel was then acquainted, that neither his promise nor his resolution should be superseded by his acceptance of the pension proposed. He had leave to be absent for a twelve-month or more, if he chose it; and to go whithersoever he pleased. On these easy conditions he thankfully accepted it.

On 16 June 1710, Handel was appointed *Kapellmeister* to the Elector of Hanover at a salary of 1,000 thaler. His insistence on his freedom to pick and choose appointments, and to accept them only on his own terms, contrasts poignantly with the experience, 60 years later, of the young Mozart, who vainly toured the courts of Europe in search of a permanent post. There were several reasons why Handel should have chosen to accept the Elector's generous offer, apart from its flexibility. Hanover had risen greatly in importance in 1692, when the newly-appointed Elector, formerly Duke Ernst August of Brunswick-Lüneburg, had selected the city as his seat. For the previous half-century, the ducal chapel had attracted many fine Italian musicians, working in both sacred and secular fields, and, in 1688, the Duke had overseen the opening of a fine new opera house, under the direction of the composer, priest and diplomat Agostino Steffani. Handel had probably met Steffani in Rome, and the older composer doubtless recommended the talented young German to the Elector. According to a conversation which Handel had with the historian Sir John Hawkins, Steffani 'took an early opportunity to introduce me [Handel] to the princess Sophia and the elector's son, giving them to understand that I was what he was pleased to call a virtuoso in music; he obliged me with instructions for my conduct and behaviour during my residence at Hanover; and being called from the city to attend to matters of a public concern, he left me in possession of that favour and patronage which himself had enjoyed for a series of years.'

The 'princess Sophia' was the Elector's mother, the Dowager Electress Sophie. She was a close friend of the eminent philosopher Leibniz (satirised by Voltaire as Dr Pangloss in *Candide*), and the Hanoverian court was famed as a centre of intellectual discussion. But despite its attractions, Handel decided almost immediately to take advantage of his year's leave. First, he returned home to Halle to see his family, where, according to Mainwaring, he had a 'melancholy interview' with his aged mother.

When he had paid his respects to his relations and friends (among whom his old master ZACKAW was by no means forgot) he set out for DÜSSELDORF. The Elector Palatine was much pleased with the punctual performance of his promise, but as much disappointed to find that he was engaged elsewhere. At parting he made him a present of a fine set of wrought plate for a desert [sic], and in such a manner as added greatly to its value.

Handel stayed only a few weeks in Düsseldorf, before travelling on through Holland towards his goal. Mainwaring continues:

It was in the winter of the year 1710, when he arrived at LONDON, one of the most memorable years of that longest, but most prosperous war... which England had ever waged with a foreign power.

Chapter 4

Music and Culture in Queen Anne's London

In 1710, the Stuart dynasty – the last of the native line – had just four years left to run. James II's daughter Queen Anne, her health sapped by gout, dropsy and the results of innumerable miscarriages and still-births, had withdrawn to the seclusion of St James's Palace. Meanwhile, the former centre of royal social life, the Palace of Whitehall – where Charles II, living up to his 'Merry Monarch' image, had once presided over a vibrant court – had burnt to the ground in 1698 and now lay blackened and roofless, a melancholy ruin on the banks of the Thames.

None-the-less, Anne's England prospered, even though her reign (1702-14) coincided with the 'first world war of modern times' – the War of the Spanish Succession. On the death of the last Spanish Hapsburg monarch, the mentally incapacitated Carlos II, both France and Austria laid claim to the Spanish throne, raising the spectre of European domination by a single power. In 1701, Great Britain, Holland, Austria, Prussia, Hanover, Portugal and Savoy formed a Grand Alliance to counteract the combined military might of Louis XIV's France and the southern German states. Under the brilliant British general John, 1st Duke of Marlborough, the Allies achieved spectacular victories at Blenheim (1704), Ramillies and Turin (1706), Oudenaarde (1708) and Malplaquet (1709); and a grateful nation rewarded Marlborough with the magnificent Blenheim Palace, built by Sir John Vanbrugh.

Meanwhile, London itself – home of one tenth of the country's population – had recovered from the ravages of the Great Fire and the devastations of plague to become a more pleasant place to live – even if its new brick buildings were quickly caked with soot from thousands of coal fires. London Bridge (which until 1738 was the only road-bridge spanning the Thames) had been handsomely rebuilt, while Wren's masterpiece had risen on the site of the old St Paul's. 15 times larger than its nearest rivals (Bristol and Norwich), London controlled the country's trade,

Queen Anne in her crown and robes. Detail from the portrait by Kneller, engraved by I. Smith.

49

sucking in food, coal and raw materials, and returning to the provinces finished goods and exotic luxuries imported from Europe, Africa, America and the Indies. The City of London – an area bounded by the Tower of London to the east, Temple Bar to the west, and Smithfield, Holborn and Whitechapel to the north – functioned as the nerve-centre of commerce. In those days, the City was far from the ghost town it now becomes at nightfall: merchants and shopkeepers lived with their families and servants above their own premises. Streets such as Old Jewry and Basinghall were reputed to house some of the country's richest men, new wealth displacing old as the aristocracy withdrew westwards to more spacious mansions around Piccadilly, Covent Garden, St James's Square and even as far north as Bloomsbury Square (one of the first London squares to be planned and developed as a coherent unit). Like the Roman cardinals, the upper classes and wealthy merchants also had their country retreats. In his *Tour through the Whole Island of Great Britain* (1724), Daniel Defoe observed, 'From Richmond to

John, 1st Duke of Marlborough in a portrait by Adriaen van der Werff.

Blenheim Palace

London, the river sides are full of villages, and those villages so full of beautiful buildings, charming gardens, and rich habitations of gentlemen of quality, that nothing in the world can imitate it; no, not the country for twenty miles around Paris.'

The lot of the poor was very different: they eked out a miserable existence in filthy, overcrowded, insanitary conditions which lasted until the slum clearance schemes of the later Victorian era. To combat the rise in drunkenness, disorder and crime, various early philanthropic societies, such as the Society for the Reformation of Manners, tried to indoctrinate the lower orders against swearing, drinking, indecency and trading – or, indeed, any activity other than church-going – on a Sunday, and persuaded the magistrates to legislate accordingly.

Up to the end of Charles II's reign, cultural activity – including music – had centred on the court. The best composers and performers, both native and foreign, had been employed by the monarch to entertain at private and official functions, to celebrate royal events, and to supply music for spectacular masques. Charles II, not wishing to be outshone by the musical glory of Louis XIV's court, had set up a royal band of 24 string players, in direct emulation of Louis' *24 Violons du roy*. Under William III and Queen Mary, many of the foreign musicians who had worked at the court were dismissed in accordance with the prevailing anti-Catholic hysteria, although eight singers and the violin band remained under the direction of Henry Purcell, who wrote several substantial odes for royal birthdays and other festive occasions. Princess Anne and her consort Prince George of

51

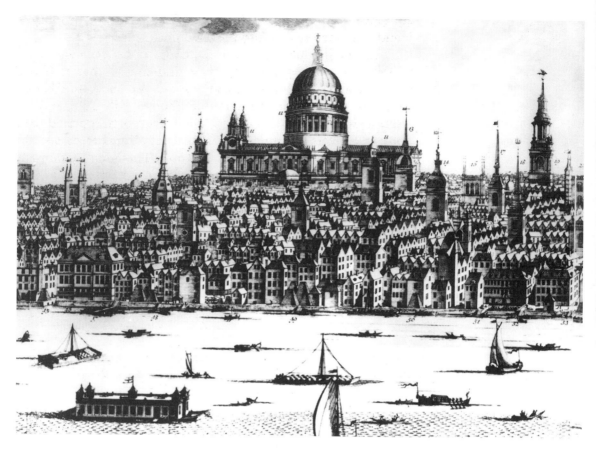

View of St Paul's Cathedral from the Thames.

Denmark also maintained a six-piece oboe band, which William and Mary borrowed for a court ball celebrating Mary's last birthday in November 1694 (she died at the end of December, followed to the grave within a year by her brilliant court composer, the brightest jewel in seventeenth-century English music).

Though not noted as an outstanding patroness of the arts, Anne was by no means unmusical. At the age of ten, she had danced in a court masque: she could sing and play the guitar, and according to the historian Sir John Hawkins, she played the harpsichord well. When she became Queen, Anne continued to employ the best musicians of the day. Her chief composer was probably the French wind player James Paisible (c.1656-1721), a former employee of James II, who had survived the subsequent purge. Anne's Master of the Music was John Eccles (c.1688-1735), while three other organist/composers – John Blow (1649-1708), William Croft (1678-1727) and Jeremiah Clarke (c.1674-1707) provided both sacred and secular works when occasion required. By the time Handel arrived in England, Blow's death and Clarke's suicide had left Croft as senior composer to the Chapel Royal, with Eccles in charge of music for entertainment. Both were competent composers, but hardly equipped to compete with their finest European contemporaries. Handel stepped neatly into the vacuum.

With the gradual decline of the court as a social centre, the performing arts began to seek new audiences. Charles II had lifted Cromwell's ban on theatres, and, in 1660, the King's Company – under the direction of Thomas Killigrew, and the Duke's Company – under Sir William Davenant, opened their doors in converted tennis courts, the first at Vere Street, and the second in Lincoln's Inn Fields. In 1663, The King's Company moved to new premises in Drury Lane (the first of several successive theatres to occupy that famous site), while eight years later, the Duke's Company moved to a newly-built theatre in Dorset Garden. In May 1682, the two companies merged as the United Company, using Drury Lane for plays, and Dorset Garden for more lavish productions with expensive scenic

The Duke's Theatre in Lincoln's Inn Fields as it appeared in the reign of Charles II.

53

effects. In 1695, some of the actors of the United Company broke away from their manager, the impresario Christopher Rich, and formed a new company under the direction of Thomas Betterton, operating from the remodelled Lincoln's Inn Fields Theatre; while Rich continued to mount rival productions at both Drury Lane and Dorset Garden.

Though run by impresarios, the theatres were controlled and financed by the aristocracy, who regularly attended performances as part of the social scene. According to a contemporary account, an average London theatre audience around 1700 consisted of 'men of Quality, particularly the younger sort, some ladies of reputation and virtue, and an abundance of damsels that hunt for prey, [who] sit all together in this place, higgledy-piggledy, chatter, toy, play, hear, hear not'. Many patrons came to be seen, rather than to see: if they left before the curtain rose, the admission charge was refunded. Since novelty was prized above intellectual content, many of the entertainments were trivial concoctions based on ludicrous plots. Music, however, was an essential component, and the theatres provided lucrative employment for singers and players. Instrumental interludes, with songs, choruses and dances, invariably introduced and concluded a play, filled in the intervals, and accompanied processions, pantomimes or battle scenes. Some was integral to the drama, but much was used simply as extra flavouring, and, by the early eighteenth century, theatre musicians were virtually giving independent concerts between the acts of plays, consisting of

Interior of the second Drury Lane Theatre seen from the stage.

Henry Purcell (1659-95).

duets or Italian trio sonatas played on violins or recorders. These 'semi-operas' did not please everybody: Roger North reported that 'some who would come to the play, hated the musick, and others that were very desirous of the musick, would not bear the interruption that so much rehearsall gave, so that it is best to have either by itself intire.'

By the last decade of the seventeenth century, this indiscriminate thirst for new music allowed a potent threat to native culture to enter by the backstage door. The first Italian singers arrived in England, and were instantly demanded by audiences, even though their offerings bore no relation at all to the dramas into which they were interpolated. In 1695, Thomas Betterton left the United Company in disgust, claiming that audiences should be able to:

> ...digest a play,
> Cooked in the plain but wholesome English way.
> 'Tis no new fashioned mess, nor flavoured strong
> With poignant sauce of dance, machine and song...
> 'Tis hard for comedy t'escape
> Without a dance, a duel, or a rape.

Within the next ten years or so, the English tradition of plays with interpolated music collapsed, in favour of spoken plays on the one hand, and opera on the other. Opera had so far failed to take root in England: Davenant's *The Siege of Rhodes* (1656), and Purcell's *Dido and Aeneas* (1689) – were more or less isolated examples. In January 1705, Thomas Clayton's Italianate *pasticcio Arsinoe, Queen of Cyprus* became the first fully through-composed 'opera' to be staged at Drury Lane. Later the same year, a magnificent new theatre, designed by Sir John Vanbrugh to accommodate anything between 900 and 2,000 spectators, and managed by himself and the dramatist William Congreve, opened in the Haymarket, conveniently close to West End aristocratic residences. The Queen's Theatre, as it was called, then housed Betterton's company, who were doubtless greatly relieved to have moved from the tiny Lincoln's Inn Fields Theatre, known popularly as 'Betterton's Booth'. The acoustics at the Queen's, with its vast empty spaces and 'immoderately high roofs' made it more suitable for singing than speaking; and the first production mounted there was a pastorale, *The Loves of Ergasto*, by the German composer Jakob Greber, sung entirely in Italian with an Italian cast.

The enterprising Christopher Rich at Drury Lane, seeing the potential of the new entertainment, soon responded with an adaptation of Bononcini's opera *Camilla*. Though *Camilla* wiped its putative English rivals off the boards, so that 'at least six or seven embryos of operas that had no being but in the airy conceptions of their pretended composers became abortive, and everyone joined in the admiration of *Camilla*' (*A Critical Discourse upon Operas in England*), it soon became clear that both companies would face bankruptcy if they each tried to produce plays and operas. In 1706, Rich staged a coup, transferring his actors to the Queen's Theatre for drama productions, while removing its theatre band to Drury Lane for a mixture of sung and spoken drama. But the musicians were unhappy: several of them – including the best wind players of the day – secretly returned to the Queen's to rehearse an opera, and were promptly dismissed by Rich 'on suspicion of being concerned in the project of acting operas in the Haymarket'. In January 1708, the situation was reversed: the singers, dancers and players were transferred back to the Queen's, leaving it with no decent actors but a fine orchestra that could apparently stand comparison with similar Continental theatre orchestras (it comprised 15 strings, a harpsichord, two oboes and three bassoons, led by the famous violinist John Banister); while Rich's Drury Lane company lacked the resources to stage even the simplest play requiring any music. This absurd situation was eventually resolved when Rich

The interior of the Queen's Theatre, Haymarket.

56

was dismissed as manager of Drury Lane, leaving both theatres free to put on a choice of entertainments.

By 1710, the year Handel arrived in London, the Queen's Theatre was giving twice-weekly opera performances. In May that year, the German visitor Uffenbach reported:

In the evening we went to the opera *Hydaspes* [by the Italian composer Francesco Mancini], which was being given for the last time, because it was summer, when the Lords for the most part reside in the country. The opera house is in Haymarket, which is a large square. It is not at all large but is certainly very massive and handsomely built. The opera was very lovely in all respects, in composition, music and representation. I am sure that, as far as the first two items are concerned, nothing could be better, even in Italy. The singers were few in number but all were excellent... The orchestra too is so well composed that it could not be better. They are all foreigners, mostly Germans and then French, for the English are not much better musicians than the Dutch, and they are fairly bad. The conductor is Pepusch from Brandenburg... The scenery and properties had all been made expressly for the opera and were very fine, though not as costly as those in Italy; but the costumes were of the finest and the performances were in all things most natural and uncommonly elegant. The singers expressed so well the emotions they must represent that I have never seen the like...

As with opera, the concept of the public concert was still relatively new to England; but, according to Hawkins, 'in proportion to the increase of wealth in the metropolis, the manners of the people began to relax; the places of public entertainment increased in number, and to these music seemed to be essential.' As a burgeoning bourgeoisie began to emerge during the latter part of the seventeenth century, a number of sharp-witted entrepreneurs discovered the 'grand secret, that the English would follow music and drop their pence freely, of which some advantage has since been made'. English concert life began, unobtrusively and unofficially, in the pub. After a period of excessive Puritanism, during which all forms of public entertainment and social activity had been prohibited, people wanted to enjoy themselves again. 'Music and wine are usually held to be such inseparable companions that the true relish of the one can never be enjoyed without the assistance of the other', wrote Ned Ward, the irrepressible 'London Spy', in 1698. After the Restoration, it became customary for impromptu musical performances to be given in London taverns, or 'music houses'. The musicians were not officially paid, but were tipped by the clientèle. Then, in 1672, the violinist John Banister the younger, advertised a series of concerts at his home in Whitefriars, opposite the George Tavern, for which (for the first time) an admission fee

Handel in a portrait by
William Hogarth.

was charged. For payment of one shilling, members of the
audience could 'call for what they pleased'. The room was
furnished with seats and small tables, 'alehouse fashion', while
clients could refresh themselves with wine, cakes and ale.

Banister's concerts were held daily (except Sunday) in Whitefriars until the beginning of 1675, when he moved first to Chandos Street in Covent Garden, and then to 'the Academy in Lincoln's Inn Fields'. His success was emulated by another group of entrepreneurs, who, in the mid-1680s, rented a concert room in Villiers Street, in a fashionable quarter between the west end of the Strand and the Thames known collectively as York Buildings, for the purpose of holding weekly public concerts. Admission for non-subscribers was 2s 6d. According to Roger North, 'there was nothing of music valued in town but was to be heard there. It was called the Music Meeting; and all the Quality and *beau mond* repaired to it.' North, however, found the concerts disorganised and lacking in focus. 'I cannot say, whatever the music was, that the entertainment was good; because it consisted of broken incoherent parts; now a consort, then a lutenist, then a violino solo, then flutes, then a song, and so piece after piece, the time sliding away...'

By the end of the seventeenth century, other venues were in regular use. These included Stationers' Hall in Ludgate Street (scene of the annual musical feast given in celebration of St Cecilia's Day by the Musical Society, for which Purcell, Blow, Clarke, and eventually, Handel, among others, provided odes in praise of the Saint), and Hickford's Room 'in Panton Street, near the Haymarket, or in James Street, over against the Tennis Court'. By 1712, Hickford's Room, which also doubled as an auction house and a dancing school, had become the principal concert hall in London, attracting a fashionable West End audience, and charging at least five shillings for entrance. A contemporary newspaper observed in 1709 that 'all ranks of people are received at plays, musical entertainments, &c, on equal terms'. As at the theatre, audiences went to concerts not only to hear music, but also to be seen, and sometimes, to indulge in rowdy behaviour: by 1711, the advertisement for a concert at Stationers' Hall hoped that 'in this consort there will be a more exact decorum than has been observed hitherto'.

Such was the state of musical life in England when Handel arrived, fuelled by his Italian successes, and eager for new conquests. According to Mainwaring:

At this time Operas were a sort of new acquaintance, but began to be established in the affections of the Nobility, many of whom had heard and admired performances of this kind in the country which gave them birth. But the conduct of them here, i.e. all that regards the drama, or plan, including also the machinery, scenes, and decorations, was foolish and absurd almost beyond imagination... The arrival of Handel put an end to this reign of nonsense.

Chapter 5

Early Years in London

Handel's reputation had preceded him. According to Mainwaring, he was soon 'introduced at Court, and honoured with the marks of the Queen's favour'. The assistant manager of the Queen's Theatre, a Swiss citizen of German descent named John Jacob Heidegger ('the most ugly man that was ever formed'), introduced the young composer into London society, which did not have long to wait for a demonstration of Handel's abilities. 'Many of the nobility were impatient for an Opera of his composing. To gratify this eagerness, RINALDO, the first he made in England, was finished in a fortnight's time' (Mainwaring). The astonishing speed of composition is attested by the librettist of the Queen's Theatre, Giacomo Rossi: his libretto was the work of 'but a few evenings', while 'Mr Hendel, the Orpheus of our century, while composing the music, scarcely gave me the time to write, and to my great wonder I saw an entire Opera put to music by that surprising genius, with the greatest degree of perfection, in only two weeks.' Rossi compiled the text from a sketch by Aaron Hill, the current manager of the Queen's Theatre. In a preface to the libretto, Hill made his aim clear:

The Deficiencies I found, or thought I found, in such ITALIAN OPERA'S as have hitherto been introduc'd among us, were, First, That they had been compos'd for Tastes and Voices, different from those who were to sing and hear them on the English Stage; And Secondly, That wanting the Machines and Decorations, which bestow so great a beauty on their Appearance, they have been heard and seen to very considerable Disadvantage.

The story of the knight Rinaldo's entanglement with the bewitching sorceress Armida is taken from Tasso's great epic poem *La Gerusalemme liberata*, a fertile source of musical inspiration since its first appearance around 1575. Lully's last full-scale opera, *Armide* (1686) is based on the same episode. In accordance with a working habit that Handel had already estab-

John Jacob Heidegger

60

lished in Italy, and which he continued throughout his career, *Rinaldo* contains a great deal of music from earlier pieces, such as the air 'Lascia ch'io pianga' from *Almira*. However, the castrato Niccolò Grimaldi (known as 'Nicolini'), in the title rôle, was given new music, including one of Handel's personal favourites, the poignant aria 'Cara sposa'.

First performed on 24 February 1711 at the Queen's Theatre, *Rinaldo* was given 15 times before the season ended on 2 June. Apart from Nicolini, the mainly Italian cast also included the male alto Valentino Urbani ('Valentini'), Isabella Girardeau as Almirena and Elisabetta Pilotti-Schiavonetti (known as 'Pilotti') as Armida. The spectacular stage effects aroused both admiration and ironic comment: Sir Richard Steele, writing in the new magazine *The Spectator* on 6 March, took great delight in pointing out technical hitches in the staging:

The King of Jerusalem is obliged to come from the City on foot, instead of being drawn in a triumphant Chariot by white Horses, as my Opera-Book had promised me; and thus while I expected Armida's Dragons should rush forward towards Argantes, I found the Hero was obliged to go to Armida, and hand her out of her Coach. We had also but a very short Allowance of Thunder and Lightning… As to the Mechanism and Scenary… the Undertakers forgetting to change their Side-Scenes, we were presented with a Prospect of the Ocean in the midst of a delightful Grove; and th'the Gentlemen on the Stage had very much contributed to the Beauty of the Grove by walking up and down between the Trees, I must own I was not a little astonished to see a well-dressed young Fellow, in a full-bottom'd Wigg, appear in the midst of the Sea, and without any visible Concern taking Snuff…

Both Steele and his fellow-journalist Joseph Addison were much amused by the production's *tour de force:* during the singing of the aria 'Augelletti' (Little Birds), accompanied behind the scenes by piccolo and two treble recorders, a flock of sparrows was released on stage to lend verisimilitude to the scene. 'There have been so many Flights of [Sparrows] let loose in this Opera, that it is feared the House will never get rid of them; and that in other Plays they may make their Entrance in very wrong and improper Scenes…besides the Inconveniences which the Heads of the Audience may sometimes suffer from them', reported Addison.

Such minor problems apart, Handel's first operatic venture for London was an indisputable success. In April, the enterprising publisher John Walsh (at that time in partnership with John Hare), issued 'All the Songs set to Musick in the last new Opera call'd Rinaldo: Together with the Symphonys and Riturnels in a Compleat Manner', which he described as having been 'exactly

Corrected' by Handel himself. It is not known whether Handel authorised the publication: Walsh was one of the most notorious 'pirates' in the business, and Handel later found it convenient to regularise their relationship in order to ensure that he, as composer, realised a share of the profits.

The month of May brought the end of the London season, and fashionable society departed to nurse its ailments at various spas and watering places, some – like Kensington, Richmond, Hampstead, Sadler's Wells in Islington, and Pancras – near to London; others – such as Tunbridge, Epsom or Bath – further afield. Defoe left a lively evocation of the spa atmosphere at Epsom Wells in the early eighteenth century:

Here you have the compliment of the place, are entered into the list of the pleasant company, so you become a citizen of Epsome for the summer; and this costs you another shilling, or, if you please, half a crown. Then you drink the waters, or walk about as if you did; dance with the ladies, though it be in your gown and slippers; have music and company of what kind you like, for every man may sort himself as he pleases; the grave with the grave, and the gay with the gay, the bright, and the wicked; all may be matched if they seek for it, and perhaps some of the last may be over-matched, if they are not upon their guard.

The spa town of Richmond in the eighteenth century.

After eight months in England, Handel too left London, for Germany. Mainwaring relates:

When he took leave of the Queen at her court, and expressed his sense of the favours conferred on him, her Majesty was pleased to add to them by large presents [yet another dinner service?], and to intimate her desire of seeing him again. Not a little flattered with such marks of approbation from so illustrious a personage, he promised to return, the moment he could obtain permission from the Prince, in whose service he was retained.

Over the next 15 months, Handel concentrated on instrumental music – concertos and overtures – for the Hanoverian court band; and a set of Italian vocal duets with *continuo* accompaniment for Princess Caroline of Ansbach (later to become Queen Caroline of England). In November 1711, he paid a visit to Halle for the baptism of his niece Johanna Friderika; and a year later, Mainwaring tells us that he 'obtained leave of the Elector to make a second visit to England, on condition that he engaged to return within a reasonable time.'

During his absence, an attempt had been made to establish opera in English by a 'gang of three', who feared the rapidly increasing popularity of Italian opera, both for its deleterious effect on native culture, and for the decline in job prospects for British singers if forced to compete with imported Italians. These three – the English composer Thomas Clayton, the Italian cellist, composer and librettist Nicola Francesco Haym, and the French composer Charles Dieupart – proposed the establishment of a series of 'Entertainments of Musick' at a house in York Buildings, at which English poetry would be set in the Italian style. 'We aim at establishing some settled Notion of what is Musick, at recovering from Neglect and Want many Families who depend upon it, at making all Foreigners who pretend to succeed in England to learn the Language of it as we ourselves have done, and not to be so insolent as to expect a whole Nation, a refined and learned Nation, should submit to learn them...' This well-meant xenophobia failed to impress: and on 5 June 1712, the last English grand opera for many years, Galliard's *Calypso and Telemachus*, was given at the Haymarket Theatre. From then on, the Italian takeover was complete.

Handel, meanwhile, had prudently taken the opportunity of learning English during his absence, and had made his first attempt at setting English words – two arias in the cantata *Venus and Adonis* by the English poet John Hughes. On his arrival back in London, he went to stay with a Mr Andrews in Barn-Elms (now Barnes). There, on 24 October 1712, he finished his next opera, based on Guarini's celebrated pastoral play *Il pastor fido* (The Faithful Shepherd). On 22 November, the refurbished Haymarket Theatre re-opened with the première of *Il pastor fido*: but even a distinguished cast (including the castrato Valeriano

Pellegrini – who had sung in *Agrippina*, Valentini, Signora Pilotti, and Margharita de l'Épine (*'La Margharita'*), who later married Pepusch) could not disguise the fact that the public, expecting something more substantial, was disappointed. As an opera diary of the period put it, 'The Scene represented only ye Country of Arcadia. ye Habits were old. ye Opera Short'. By 10 December, it had been superseded by a new *pasticcio*, *Dorinda*. Nine days later, Handel completed his next work, *Teseo*, to a text by Haym.

Teseo – the story of Theseus's rivalry with Aegeus (who, unknown to both, is his father) for the love of the princess Agilea, further complicated by the sorceress Medea's destructive passion for Theseus – was based on the French libretto which Jean-Philippe Quinault had provided for Lully in 1675: in accordance with its French original, it is Handel's only five-act opera. In his *General History of Music*, Burney provides an extended critique of *Teseo*, which again featured Pellegrini in the title rôle, Pilotti as Medea, supported by Margharita de l'Épine and Valentini. Burney was particularly impressed by the musical characterisation of 'the enraged Medea': her aria 'O stringerò nel sen' he found 'full of fire and dramatic effects'; while her 'wild and savage fury' and her 'incantations' were 'admirably painted by the instruments' in an accompanied recitative at the conclusion of Act Three.

Teseo, premièred on 10 January 1713, was a great success, running for 13 nights. Disaster struck on the second night, when the theatre manager, Owen Swiney, fled to Italy with the box-office receipts. 'Mr Swiny Brakes & runs away, & leaves ye Singers unpaid ye Scenes & Habits also unpaid for. The Singers were in Some confusion but at last concluded to go on with ye

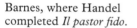

Barnes, where Handel completed *Il pastor fido*.

operas on their own accounts, & divide ye Gain amongst them.' The appropriately-named Swiney was promptly replaced by Handel's friend Heidegger.

Meanwhile, Handel had found a new patron in the 19-year-old Richard Boyle, Earl of Burlington, who offered him accommodation in his Piccadilly residence. According to Hawkins:

Into this hospitable mansion was Handel received, and left at liberty to follow the dictates of his genius and invention, assisting frequently at evening concerts, in which his own music made the most considerable part. The course of his studies during three years residence at Burlington-house, was very regular and uniform: his mornings were employed in study, and at dinner he sat down with men of the first eminence for genius and abilities of any in the kingdom.

This distinguished company included men of letters, architects and painters, among whom were the poets Alexander Pope and John Gay, the Queen's physician Dr John Arbuthnot (a noted wit and satirist), and the designer William Kent. Gay's *Trivia: or, The Art of Walking the Streets of London* paints a lively picture of this temple of culture:

Yet *Burlington's* fair Palace still remains;
Beauty within, without Proportion reigns.
Beneath his Eye declining Art revives,
The Wall with animated Picture lives;
There *Hendel* strikes the Strings, the melting Strain
Transports the Soul, and thrills through ev'ry Vein;
There oft I enter (but with cleaner Shoes)
For *Burlington's* belov'd by ev'ry Muse.

John Gay (1685-1732)

Burlington House, Piccadilly, in 1700.

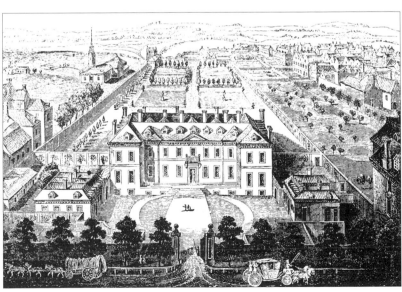

Alexander Pope (1688-1744).

According to Mainwaring, Pope remained unmoved by Handel's skill at the harpsichord, declaring that 'his ears were of that untoward make, and reprobate cast, as to receive his Music, which he was persuaded was the best that could be, with as much indifference as the airs of a common ballad.' However, 'the Poet one day asked his friend Dr ARBUTHNOT, of whose knowledge in Music he had a high idea, what was his real opinion in regard to Handel as a Master of that Science? The Doctor immediately replied, "Conceive the highest that you can of his abilities, and they are much beyond any thing that you can conceive".'

Handel also renewed his court connections; for Queen Anne's birthday on 6 February he supplied an ode in the Purcellian tradition. His reward was a royal commission to celebrate the signing of the Treaty of Utrecht, which, on 31 March 1713, brought the War of the Spanish Succession to a satisfactory end. The Spanish empire was partitioned: Spain and many of her colonies went to Philip of Anjou, Louis XIV's grandson, whom Carlos II had named as his heir; Austria secured territories in Europe; and Great Britain, who now found herself holding the balance of world power, acquired Gibraltar, Minorca, Newfoundland, Nova Scotia, territories in the Hudson Bay area and the monopoly of the slave trade with Latin America. Such important national events were customarily marked by the performance of a *Te Deum* and *Jubilate*; settings by Purcell had been performed since 1694 in St Paul's Cathedral on state occasions. But, as Mainwaring puts it, 'had our musicians been thought equal to the task, a foreigner would hardly have been applied to for the song of triumph and thanksgiving, which was

Handel in a portrait by Phillipp Mercier.

now wanted.' In anticipation of the peace, Handel completed a *Te Deum* on 13 January, and a *Jubilate* some time shortly afterwards. Both were performed, with native-born singers, at the official thanksgiving service at St Paul's on 7 July 1713. Although the Queen did not attend the service, she rewarded the composer with a life annuity of £200, 'as a testimony of her regard to his merit'.

At the beginning of June, a new opera by Handel was performed either at the Queen's Theatre or privately at Burlington House. Little is known about *Silla*, to a libretto by Rossi: it seems to have had only a single performance, and much of the music reappeared in his next opera, *Amadigi*. Meanwhile, Handel's leave of absence from Hanover had expired. According to Mainwaring:

The time had again elapsed to which the leave he had obtained, could in reason be extended. But whether he was afraid of repassing the sea, or whether he had contracted an affection for the diet of the land he was in; so it was, that the promise he had given at his coming away, had somehow slipt out of his memory.

Handel's memory must have received a rude jolt when Queen Anne died childless on 1 August 1714; her successor was none other than his employer, the Elector of Hanover – now, thanks to the 1701 Act of Settlement, King George I of England. According to Mainwaring:

HANDEL, conscious of how ill he had deserved at the hands of his gracious patron...did not dare to shew himself at court. To account for his delay in returning to his office, was no easy matter. To make an excuse for the non-performance of his promise, was impossible. From this ugly situation he was soon relieved by better luck than he deserved. It happened that his noble friend Baron KILMANSECK [Kielmansegge] was here. He, with some others among the nobility, contrived a method for reinstating him in the favour of his Majesty... The King was persuaded to form a party on the water. HANDEL was apprised of the design, and advised to prepare some Music for that occasion. It was performed and conducted by himself, unknown to his Majesty, whose pleasure on hearing it was equal to his surprise. He was impatient to know whose it was, and how this entertainment came to be provided without his knowledge. The Baron then produced the delinquent, and asked leave to present him to his Majesty, as one that was too conscious of his fault to attempt an excuse for it; but sincerely desirous to attone for the same by all possible demonstrations of duty, submission, and gratitude, could he but hope that his Majesty, in his great goodness, would be pleased to accept them. This intercession was accepted without any difficulty. HANDEL was restored to favour, and his Music honoured with the highest expressions of the royal approbation.

George I of England, formerly Elector of Hanover.

This account – the origin of the famous *Water Music* – cannot be authenticated; and it is now generally believed that the river trip, during which the *Water Music* was undoubtedly played, took place three years later. None-the-less, Handel's disgrace was evidently short-lived; on 26 September, a *Te Deum* and anthem by him were sung during a service at the Chapel Royal, attended by the King.

On 25 May 1715, Handel's new opera *Amadigi* – 'All the Cloaths and Scenes entirely New. With variety of Dancing...' –

The hornpipe from the *Water Music* in the composer's hand.

opened at the Haymarket theatre, now renamed the King's. Dedicated to the Earl of Burlington, the libretto was another of Haym's adaptations of Quinault (originally for Lully's *Amadis* of 1684), and, once again, is a drama of sexual jealousy (the eponymous hero is loved by the faithful Oriana, and also by the sorceress Melissa, who does all she can to win Amadis, by fair means or foul). A fully operational fountain was just one of *Amadigi*'s spectacular stage effects: indeed an advertisement in the *Daily Courant* advised 'And whereas there is a great many Scenes and Machines to be mov'd in this Opera, which cannot be done if Persons should stand upon the Stage (where they could not be without Danger), it is therefore hop'd no Body, even the Subscribers, would take it Ill that they must be deny'd Entrance on the Stage.' Though it boasted a strong cast (Nicolini in the title rôle, Pilotti as Melissa, and two new singers – Anastasia Robinson as Oriana and the contralto Diana Vico in the male rôle of Dardano), *Amadigi* had a disappointingly short run of seven performances, interrupted by the King's birthday (on which there was no opera), the excessive midsummer heat and the indisposition and subsequent withdrawal of Mrs Robinson. On 23 July, the season came to a premature close, due to the first

Anastasia Robinson, later
Countess of Peterborough.

Jacobite rebellion ('ye Rebellion of ye Tories and Papists', which attempted to restore the Stuart dynasty), as a result of which the Court remained indoors, 'not liking to go into such Crowds these troublesome times'.

Although the theatres remained closed for the rest of the year, Handel had still made enough money out of his successes to date – particularly from *Rinaldo*, which had been constantly revived – to invest £500 in the notorious South Sea Company (whose Bubble finally burst in 1720). In June 1716, he requested the withdrawal of his dividend, presumably to finance his forthcoming trip to Germany. King George left for Hanover on 7 July, and Handel followed him a few days later. He visited his family in Halle, and then went on to Ansbach, where he met an old friend from his student days who subsequently played a major, though unobtrusive rôle in his life. Handel persuaded the wool merchant Johann Christoph Schmidt to give up his trade, anglicise his name to plain John Christopher Smith, and return with him to London as his treasurer and copyist, bringing with him his four-year-old son, Johann Christoph Jr, who took over the same function on his father's death.

At some point during the six months he spent in Germany, Handel is thought to have set B.H. Brockes's famous Passion oratorio text, closely associated with Hamburg (where his more recent operas were beginning to achieve performances) and set around the same period by many notable Hamburg composers, including Keiser, Telemann and Mattheson. Mattheson thought that Handel's version was composed in England, and sent by post to Hamburg. It may have been performed there in 1716; but the first documented performance took place in the refectory of Hamburg Cathedral on 23 March 1719. In *The New Grove*, Winton Dean considers that the work was 'not an artistic success. Unlike Bach, who used many of Brockes's verses in his St John Passion, Handel was not inspired by the sentimental imagery of German Pietism'.

Chapter 6

Cannons

George the First knew nothing, and desired to know nothing; did nothing, and desired to do nothing; and the only good thing that is told of him is, that he wished to restore the crown to its hereditary successor. (Dr Johnson)

The accession of George I inaugurated a century of what many consider to have been Britain's cultural golden age – the Georgian period. Under four successive Hanoverian monarchs, a broad-based social aristocracy, including noblemen, squires, wealthy clergymen and the educated middle classes, sought improvements in the quality of their lives. Graceful, classically-proportioned terraces and crescents inspired by the study of the Ancient World began to adorn Britain's cities, replacing the Dutch-influenced redbrick of William III and Queen Anne; while in the countryside, Capability Brown's designer landscapes encircled magnificent stately homes, decorated by Adam and

Royal Crescent, Bath, taken from the park in an engraving after W. Hardwick.

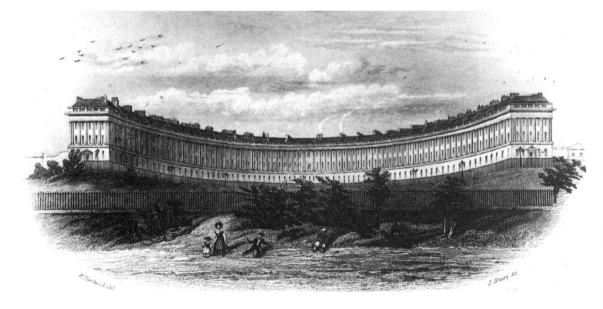

Roubiliac, and filled with the exquisite artifacts of Chippendale and Sheraton. A solid programme of road-building, combined with improvements in conveyances themselves, made travel easier and communication better: in the 1720s, Defoe set off on his memorable tour of Great Britain, while all young gentlemen were encouraged to take the Grand European Tour to complete their educations. This elegant, courtly, pre-Industrial Revolution world, where everyone 'knew his proper station', is captured in the aristocratic portraits of Gainsborough, Reynolds and Zoffany; while in the clubs and coffee houses of London, the keenest literary minds of the day – Pope, Gay, Smollett, Swift, Viscount Bolingbroke, and later Goldsmith, Johnson and Boswell, among others – discussed issues of the day and evolved their witty epigrams. In 1719, Defoe published his *Robinson Crusoe*, followed three years later by *Moll Flanders*; Swift's *Gulliver's Travels* appeared in 1726; while one of the fathers of the modern novel, Samuel Richardson, published *Pamela; or Virtue Rewarded* in 1740, and his masterpiece, *Clarissa* in 1748, followed a year later by Henry Fielding's *Tom Jones*.

For the fortunate few, it was an age of prosperity, security and achievement. The poor, meanwhile, were regarded by those in authority with appalling complacency. Parliament consisted entirely of the aristocracy and the landed gentry, who could be relied upon to look after their own interests at the expense of a disenfranchised under-class. During the 1720s, the widespread consumption of gin by the poor (shamefully encouraged by de-regulation of supply and under-taxation to protect landed interests) accounted for at least 20 per cent of the London adult death rate: its devastating effects were graphically depicted in Hogarth's famous cartoon *Gin Lane*. Judicial punishments were harsh, particularly where property was concerned: stealing anything – even so little as a handkerchief – was punishable by death; while in the squalid debtors' prisons brutal jailors tortured the unfortunate inmates to death in fruitless efforts to extract unpayable fees. Encouraged by the efforts of social reformers, and shocked by Hogarth's vivid depictions of poverty and despair, a new spirit of philanthropy had gained ground by the 1740s: voluntary subscriptions raised money for the establishment of hospitals such as Guy's, Westminster, St George's, London and Middlesex in the capital, together with lying-in (maternity) and county hospitals in the principal towns; while a new sense of pity and responsibility for the thousands of children growing up in neglect and disease eventually led to the establishment of charity and Sunday schools. Such philanthropy, which received a new boost by the spreading influence of 'Methodism', as opposed to the class-ridden High Anglicanism of the Church of England,

Gin Lane by William Hogarth.

was still, however, seen as a useful tool in the subordination of the lower classes: if people were decently fed and housed, they would be less likely to foment dangerous revolutionary principles which might threaten the social order of the day.

Such was the social structure in which Handel spent the last four and a half decades of his life. He witnessed the beginning of the Georgian era, and died a year before the accession of George III. His first Hanoverian patron, the 'honest blockhead' George I, was not popular with his British subjects. His reluctance to adapt to English customs – or even to learn the language – did little to earn him respect, while his family life was the subject of much scandalised gossip. George ignored his wife, appeared in public with his German mistress, Baroness von der Schulenberg (known as 'The Maypole'), and openly despised his eldest son, the Prince of Wales. George was, however, fond of entertainment: as well as regular opera-going, he enjoyed the elaborate masquerades which

74

the impresario Heidegger put on each winter, in his capacity as 'the cleverest purveyor of entertainments to the Nobility'.

In July 1717 the King expressed a desire to have a concert on the river, partly as a public relations exercise. Since Heidegger declined to organise the event on the grounds that he could not afford the substantial costs, it fell to the long-suffering Baron Kielmansegge to placate his angry monarch by offering not only to make the necessary arrangements, but also to foot the bill. According to a report sent back to Berlin by Friedrich Bonet, the Prussian Ambassador to London:

About eight in the evening the King repaired to His barge, into which were admitted the Duchess of Bolton, Countess Godolphin, Mad. de Kilmanseck, Mrs Were and the Earl of Orkney, the Gentleman of the Bedchamber in Waiting. Next to the King's barge was that of the musicians, about 50 in number, who played on all kinds of instruments, to wit trumpets, horns, hautboys, bassoons, German flutes, French flutes, violins and basses; but there were no singers. The music had been composed specially by the famous Handel, a native of Halle, and His Majesty's Principal Court Composer. His Majesty approved of it so greatly that he caused it to be repeated three times in all, although each performance lasted an hour – namely twice before and once after supper. The evening was all that could be desired for the festivity, the number of barges and above all of boats filled with people desirous of hearing was beyond counting. In order to make this entertainment the more exquisite, Mad. de Kilmanseck had arranged a choice supper in the late Lord Ranelagh's villa at Chelsea on the river, where the King went at one in the morning. He left at three o'clock and returned to St James's about half past four. The concert cost Baron Kilmanseck [sic]

A public execution before the Debtors' Door of Newgate Prison.

The Physick Garden,
Chelsea, from the river.

£150 for the musicians alone. Neither the Prince nor the Princess [of Wales] took any part in this festivity.

Handel's famous *Water Music*, an attractive mixture of ceremony and pure entertainment, comprises three suites: one in F major, scored for oboes, bassoons, horns and strings; another in D, for the same instruments plus trumpets; and one in G, scored for flutes, recorders or oboes, plus bassoons. Roger Fiske has suggested that the F major suite may have been written for the 1714 water party (if it ever took place); while movements from it and the D major suite probably accompanied the 1717 expedition. The subdued scoring of the G major suite would clearly render it unsuitable for open-air performance, and Fiske suggests that it may have been played to accompany the King's supper at Chelsea. In style, the work is a mixture of Italian-type concerto movements and French-style dances including bourrées and hornpipes: it represents the first use of horns combined with trumpets in English orchestral music.

Meanwhile, *Rinaldo* and *Amadigi* had both enjoyed revivals at the King's Theatre throughout the spring; however, at the end of June the theatre closed, and did not reopen for opera performances for another three years. Not satisfied with his court duties, which included teaching the royal princesses (for which he now received an annual salary of £600) and the King's illegitimate daughter by 'The Maypole', Handel cast around for another post. During the summer he entered the service of James Brydges, Earl of Carnarvon and, from 1719, Duke of Chandos. In his capacity as Paymaster-General to the British armies during Marlborough's campaigns, Brydges had done rather well for himself, increasing his private fortune by over half a million pounds. In 1713, he had acquired a country residence about ten miles north of London, at Cannons, near Edgware in Middlesex. Over the next decade, the house was remodelled in grand Palladian style, principally under the direction of Vanbrugh. 83 acres of grounds were laid out with splendid lawns and terraces, Italian formal gardens, ornamental ponds and canals, groves and walks, 'wildernesses', fruit, vegetable and herb gardens; all inhabited by a range of exotic wildlife including storks, macaws, flamingos, eagles and Virgina deer. In 1725, Defoe visited Cannons, and declared it to be:

An artist's impression of Handel sailing on the Thames with King George I, listening to the *Water Music*.

a most magnificent palace or mansion house, I might say, the most magnificent in England. This palace is so beautiful in its situation, so lofty, so majestic the appearance of it, that a pen can but ill describe it, the pencil not much better... The fronts are all of freestone, the columns

James Brydges, First Duke of Chandos.

and pilasters are lofty and beautiful, the windows very high, with all possible ornaments. No ornament is wanting to make it the finest house in England. The plastering and gilding is done by the famous Pargotti an Italian... The great salon or hall is painted by Paolucci, for the Duke spared no cost to have every thing as rich as possible. The pillars supporting the building are all of marble: the great staircase is the finest by far of any in England; and the steps are all of marble, every step being of one whole piece, about 22 foot in length. The inside of this house is as glorious, as the outside is fine; the lodgings are indeed most exquisitely finished, and if I may call it so, royally furnished... In a word, no nobleman in England, and very few in Europe, lives in greater splendour, or maintains a grandeur or magnificence, equal to the Duke of Chandos... Here are continually maintained, and that in the dearest part in England, as to house expenses, not less than one hundred and twenty in family...every servant in the house is made easy, and his life comfortable; and they have the felicity that it is their lord's desire and delight that it should be so.

John Christopher Pepusch in a portrait by an unknown artist.

Although the building work was not yet complete in 1717, Brydges had already assembled a private chapel of musicians, under the musical direction of the German composer Pepusch. By the time Handel arrived as composer-in-residence, the Cannons musical establishment consisted of between four and six violins, two cellos, one trumpet, one bassoon, one keyboard player, three woodwind players proficient on transverse flute, oboe and recorder, and about nine singers. Despite the dangerous precedents of Cardinal Wolsey in Henry VIII's England, and – more recently – Nicholas Fouquet in Louis XIV's France, Brydges was clearly determined to live in royal style, emulating or even outshining his monarch's lifestyle. According to Defoe:

The chapel is a singularity, not only in its building, and the beauty of its workmanship, but in this also: that the Duke maintains there a full choir, and has the worship perform'd there with the best music, after the manner of the Chapel Royal, which is not done in any other noble man's Chapel in Britain; no not the Prince of Wales's, though heir apparent to the Crown. Nor is the chapel only furnish'd with such excellent musick, but the Duke has a set of them to entertain him every day at dinner'.

As usual, Handel wasted little time settling down to work. On 25 September 1717, Brydges informed Dr Arbuthnot that 'Mr Handle has made me two new Anthems very noble ones, & most think they far exceed the first two. He is at work for 2 more, & some Overtures to be plaied before the first lesson. You had as good take Cannons in your way to London.'

Altogether, Handel composed 11 anthems (since known as

Cannons, the residence of the Duke of Chandos.

79

Title page of the first edition
of *Acis and Galatea*, published
by John Walsh.

the *Chandos Anthems*) for Cannons in his first year there (one,
O be Joyful, was an arrangement of the *Utrecht Jubilate*). Their style
owes much to Purcell, with inevitable Italian influence. Since the
chapel at Cannons was not completed until 1720, it is believed
that these works were performed at the nearby church of St
Lawrence – the only part of the vast estate which still exists.
Cannons – which cost Brydges nearly a quarter of a million
pounds – was demolished around 1747, a mere 20 years after its
completion.

As well as the *Chandos Anthems* and a *Te Deum*, Handel wrote two other major works for Cannons: both settings of English words. The masque *Acis and Galatea*, to a libretto by Handel's Burlington friends, including Gay, Pope and John Hughes, was performed at Cannons in May 1718, probably with some elementary staging. Compared with Handel's earlier setting of the same tale (from Ovid's *Metamorphoses*), the characterisation of the three protagonists is developed far more convincingly and movingly: the 'monster Polypheme' even inspires a certain amount of sympathy in his hopeless attempts at bucolic gallantry ('O ruddier than the cherry'), while the death of Acis is handled with true pathos. *Esther*, based on Pope and Arbuthnot's adaptation of Racine's great tragedy – itself taken from the Old Testament story – was the first English oratorio, in the sense of a biblical drama set to music without staging. The success of its public revival in 1732 was to change the course of Handel's career, and to some extent, of English music. The original date of composition is unknown, but 1718 seems the most likely.

In August that year, Handel's sister died in Halle, and, six months later, he wrote to his bereaved brother-in-law, apologising for not having visited the family sooner. 'It is greatly to my regret that I find myself kept here by affairs of the greatest moment, on which (I venture to say) all my fortunes depend; but they have continued much longer than I had anticipated'. These 'affairs' are amplified by Mainwaring:

During the last year of his residence at Cannons, a project was formed by the Nobility for erecting an academy at the Haymarket. The intention of this musical Society, was to secure to themselves a constant supply of Operas to be composed by Handel, and performed under his direction. For this end a subscription was set on foot: and as his...Majesty was pleased to let his name appear at the head of it, the Society was dignified with the title of the Royal Academy. The sum subscribed being very large, it was intended to continue for fourteen years certain. But as yet it was in its embrio-state, being not fully formed till a year or two after.

Chapter 7

The Royal Academy of Music

By 21 February 1719, Handel had left Cannons after his two-year absence from London society. Three months later, the embryonic Royal Academy of Music, intended for the 'Encouragement of Operas', had acquired 62 subscribers, under the governorship of the Lord Chamberlain – Thomas Holles, Duke of Newcastle. The list of patrons willing to invest in such a speculative venture included dukes, earls, viscounts and marquesses, among them both of Handel's noble patrons, the Duke of Chandos and the Earl of Burlington; while the King himself guaranteed an 'annuity or Yearly Bounty' of £1,000. Each subscriber, or shareholder, put up at least £200 to create a 'joint stock' of £10,000 (in fact, the total sum subscribed seems to have been much larger – anywhere between £16,000 and £20,000); and the investors were promised a fanciful 25 per cent return on their capital. The management of the company was placed in the competent hands of Heidegger, with the Italian Paolo Rolli as chief librettist and another Italian, Roberto Clerici, as designer. Handel, as 'Master of Musick', was authorised 'to repair to Italy, Germany or such other Place or Places as you shall think proper, there to make Contracts with such Singer or Singers as you shall judge fit to perform on the English Stage'. In particular, he was instructed to 'engage Senezino [the famous castrato Bernardi Francesco Senesino] as soon as possible to Serve the said Company and for as many Years as may be.'

Handel duly set out, first for Düsseldorf, then for a brief family visit to Halle, and on to the Elector of Saxony's court at Dresden, where many of the best Italian singers, including Senesino, were currently engaged. In Dresden, Handel performed for the King, and heard *Teofane*, a new opera by Lotti, performed in September to celebrate the marriage of the Elector's son. (Three years later, Handel used an adaptation of the same libretto for his own *Ottone*.) On 15 July, he informed the Earl of Burlington that he was 'waiting for the engagements of Sinesino[sic], Berselli and

Handel at the harpsichord; portrait by Thornhill.

Guizzardi [sic] to be concluded'. In fact, Senesino – whose current salary was an astronomical 7,000 thalers – proved a difficult catch to land; and his engagement (for 2,000 guineas) was not concluded until the following year, when both he and the tenor Matteo Berselli joined the company. Guicciardi never came to England; and the only Dresden singer whom Handel managed to procure for the Royal Academy's first season was Margherita Durastanti, who had sung the title rôle in his *Agrippina* in Venice ten years earlier. Paolo Rolli greeted the news of her appointment with derision. 'Oh! what a bad choice for England! I shall not enter into her singing merits but she really is an Elephant!'

By 30 November 1719, the Board of Directors of the Royal Academy – who included Dr Arbuthnot, Colonel John Blaithwaite (a former musical prodigy who had studied with Alessandro Scarlatti), the Earl of Burlington and Sir John Vanbrugh – had formally appointed Handel, in his absence, 'Master of the Orchestra with a Sallary' (his orchestra was to consist of 34 of the best players in London). They also decided to entice the Italian composer Bononcini to London 'for composing and performing in the Orchestra'. Heidegger engaged the tenor Benedetto Baldassari – his wife, the contralto Catterina Galerati, and the experienced English soprano Anastasia Robinson. Within a few months, a sufficient cast had been assembled for the new opera company to open in Giovanni Porta's *Numitore* at the King's Theatre on 2 April 1720. Just over three weeks later, on 27 April, Handel's *Radamisto*, with only three Italian singers (Durastanti in the title rôle, Galerati as Tigrane and Baldassari as Fraarte) out of an otherwise native cast, had its triumphant première in the presence of the King, his 'ladies' (his mistress and her daughter), and the Prince of Wales. The demand for tickets was so great that the management was obliged to put extra seats on the stage itself, at a guinea a time. 'If persons… who were present at that performance may be credited, the applause it received was almost as extravagant as his AGRIPPINA had excited: the crowds and tumults of the house at VENICE were hardly equal to those at LONDON', reported Mainwaring…

In so splendid and fashionable an assembly of ladies (to the excellence of their taste we must impute it) there was no shadow of form, or ceremony, scarce indeed any appearance of order or regularity, politeness or decency. Many, who had forc'd their way into the house with an impetuosity but ill suited to their rank and sex, actually fainted through the excessive heat and closeness of it. Several gentlemen were turned back, who had offered forty shillings for a seat in the gallery, after having despaired of getting any in the pit or boxes.

Handel dedicated his score – a drama of sexual jealousy and marital virtue set during the reign of the Roman Emperor Claudius – to the King, who returned the compliment by granting Handel a royal copyright privilege for a 14-year term. Such privileges had been common from the Elizabethan period until 1636, when Charles I abolished them: the Copyright Act of 1709 had revived the practice, although most publishers openly flouted the law. Handel, like other composers of his day, suffered greatly from breaches of copyright: while the complete score of an opera could be entrusted to a single publisher, no one could stop an unscrupulous rival from obtaining copies of individual popular numbers (known as 'favourite songs'), and selling them in various pirated formats, including instrumental arrangements – for which the composer received no money. In fact, the royal licence granted to Handel 'strictly forbidding all our loving Subjects within our Kingdoms and Dominions, to Reprint or Abridge the same, either in the like, or any other Volume or Volumes whatsoever, or to Import, Buy, Vend, Utter or Distribute any Copies thereof Reprinted beyond the Seas, during the aforesaid Term of Fourteen Years' quickly proved unenforceable. The second edition of Handel's harpsichord lessons, suites of dance movements 'intermix'd with fugues' composed 'for the practice of the princess Anne' (the last movement in the E major suite is the famous *Harmonious Blacksmith*), published in November 1720, carried an author's note:

I have been obliged to publish some of the following Lessons, because surrepticious and incorrect Copies of them had got Abroad [these refer to pirated editions then circulating, issued in Amsterdam by the respectable firms of Jeanne Roger and Michel Charles Le Cène]. I have added several new Ones to make the Work more usefull, which if it meets with a favourable Reception; I will still proceed to publish more, reckoning it my duty, with my Small Talent, to serve a Nation from which I have receiv'd so Generous a protection.

In the summer of 1720, the collapse of the 'South Sea Bubble', a disastrous foray into joint-stock trading, brought economic ruin to many of its unfortunate investors. Handel too, lost money. According to Paolo Rolli: 'The whole nobility is at its last gasp; only gloomy faces are to be seen. Great bankers are going bankrupt, great shareholders just disappear and there is not an acquaintance or friend who has escaped total ruin. These rogues of Company Directors have betrayed everybody and I assure you the tragic worst is feared.' Amid this general economic distress, the Royal Academy (many of whose noble patrons had invested in South Sea shares and now found themselves financially embarrassed and unable to pay their 'calls', or regular

An Emblematical Print on the South Sea Scheme by William Hogarth, 1721.

subscriptions) prepared its autumn season. Margherita Durastanti declared herself pregnant, much to the annoyance of the directors; but, at the end of September, Senesino finally arrived in London, together with Berselli and the second soprano Maddalena Salvai.

Although flatteringly described by his admirer Rolli as 'a man well-mannered, well-read, extremely kind and endowed with the noblest sentiments', Senesino had been dismissed from Dresden for refusing to sing an aria which displeased him and tearing up another singer's music. He and the equally short-tempered Handel crossed swords almost immediately over the singer's proposed début in the revival of an existing opera. Senesino, who naturally wished to show off his brilliant technique in newly-composed music, rather than 'a pastiche of old arias', objected; and Handel called him 'a damned Fool'. Eventually, two directors, Arbuthnot and Blaithwaite, were called in to smooth things over; but relations between singer and composer remained mistrustful. According to Hawkins:

Handel was not a proud man, but he was capricious: in his comparison of the merits of a composer and those of a singer, he estimated the latter at a very low rate, and affected to treat Senesino with a degree of indifference that the other could but ill brook; in short, they were upon very ill terms almost from the moment of their first coming together; but in a year or two…the flame of civil discord burst forth, and all was disorder and confusion.

None-the-less, Senesino was an indisputable ornament to the Royal Academy. 'The stage was never so well served as it is now, there is not one indifferent voice, they are all Italians', wrote Mary Pendarves (later Delany, a lifelong friend and supporter of Handel). 'There is one man called Serosini [Senesino] who is beyond Nicolini both in person and voice.' '[Senesino] had a powerful, clear, equal and sweet contralto voice, with a perfect intonation and an excellent shake', wrote the German theorist Quantz. 'His manner of singing was masterly and his elocution unrivalled… His countenance was well adapted to the stage, and the action was natural and noble. To these qualities he joined a majestic figure.'

The Royal Academy's second season opened with *Astarto* by Bononcini, who had also recently arrived in London. Its success (it had an unprecedented run of 24 performances) did not augur well for cordial relations between Bononcini and Handel. In December, *Radamisto* was revived with a great deal of new music, with Senesino in the title rôle, and Durastanti (the original Radamisto) as Zenobia. The King and other members of the royal family attended, but although Senesino performed 'with his wonted Applause', the opera ran only for seven nights. According to Mainwaring, the directors of the Academy decided to settle the incipient rivalry between its three house composers (the third, the cellist Filippo Amadei – Handel's former colleague from his days in the Ruspoli household – was shortly to be replaced by Attilio Ariosti), by inviting each to submit one act of a composite opera: 'And he, who by the general suffrage, should be allowed to have given the best proofs of his abilities, was to be put into possession of the house.' The opera was *Muzio Scevola*, to a text by Rolli; and according to Mainwaring, 'The event was answerable to the expectations of Handel's friends. His act was the last, and the superiority of it so very manifest, that there was not the least pretence for any further doubts or disputes.' Although such competitions were not uncommon (20 years earlier, several 'persons of quality' had sponsored a musical *Judgment of Paris*, for which four of the best composers of the day had submitted settings of Congreve's masque of that title), it seems unlikely that the Academy would have risked alienating two of its composers through an ill-judged 'contest', and composite operas were common practice in Italy. Nevertheless, Mainwaring's insistence on the competitive element seems to have been vindicated by contemporary opinion, which decided that Handel had 'easily triumphed over the others'. *Muzio Scevola,* however, was not a success. John Gay provided a mocking epitaph:

> Who here blames words, or verses, songs, or singers,
> Like Mutius Scaevola will burn his fingers.

Despite its teething problems and personality clashes, the new company was now up and running. According to Mainwaring:

all things went on prosperously for a course of...years. And this may justly be called the period of musical glory, whether we consider the performances or the performers, most certainly not to be surpassed, if equalled, in any age or country... The perfect authority which Handel maintained over the singers and the band, or rather the total subjection in which he held them, was of more consequence than can well be imagined. It was the chief means of preserving that order and decorum, that union and tranquillity, which seldom are found to subsist for any long continuance in musical Societies.

The Academy's third season opened on 1 November 1721 with a series of revivals and three new operas, Handel's *Floridante* (9 December), Bononcini's *Crispo* (10 January 1722), and *Griselda,* also by Bononcini (22 February). To Handel's chagrin, Bononcini's works enjoyed consistently longer runs than his own; and when the nation's hero, the Duke of Marlborough, died in June 1722, it was Bononcini who was invited to compose the anthem for his state funeral. Two years later, when Bononcini announced that he was going to leave England, the Duchess of Marlborough settled £500 per annum on him 'to oblige him to continue here'. Although he was not engaged by the Academy for its autumn 1722 season, and from then onwards wrote few operas for the company, Handel continued to regard Bononcini as a threat: in 1725, an 'Epigram on the Feuds Between Handel and Bononcini' by the poet and wit John Byrom was published in the newspapers, to the great amusement of London society.

> Some say, compar'd to Bononcini
> That Mynheer Handel's but a Ninny;
> Others aver, that he to Handel
> Is scarcely fit to hold a Candle:
> Strange all this Difference should be
> 'Twixt Tweedle-dum and Tweedle-dee!

In the eyes of the public, the two composers' styles were complementary: Handel 'would furnish us with Airs expressive of the Rage of Tyrants, the Passions of Heroes, and the Distress of Lovers in the Heroick Stile', while Bononcini 'soothes us with sighing Shepherds, bleating Flocks, chirping Birds, and purling Streams in the Pastoral'. Burney was less charitable: 'After the performance or perusal of an opera by Bononcini or Attilio [Ariosti], the proceeding to one of Handel's, is going from Arabia Petrea to Arabia Felix; from barren rocks to spontaneous fertility.' None-the-less, Bononcini's fluently melodious style evidently pleased the public, and several commentators have noted that Handel tried to amend his style to compete with his rival – in particular, by curbing his tendency to write excessively long and elaborate arias. Bononcini remained in London until the revelation of a flagrant act of plagiarism at the Academy of Ancient Musick, of which he was a founder member (he claimed authorship of a madrigal actually by Antonio Lotti), obliged him to leave the country in 1732.

Handel's next opera, *Ottone*, whose plot concerned the marriage of the German king Otto II, was ready by August 1722, but took three months – an inordinately long time by his standards – to reach the stage. On 27 October, the *London Journal* reported:

There is a new Opera now in Rehearsal at the Theatre in the Hay-Market, a Part of which is reserv'd for one Mrs *Cotsona* [Cuzzoni], an extraordinary Italian Lady, who is expected daily from Italy. It is said, she has a much finer Voice and more accurate Judgment, than any of her Country Women who have performed on the English Stage.

Francesca Cuzzoni, the toast of Italy, arrived in England at the end of the year. Her fee was huge – £2,000 a season – but even the most expensive and temperamental of *prime donne* met their match in Handel. During the rehearsals of *Ottone*, Cuzzoni reportedly refused to sing the aria 'Falsa imagine'. Handel promptly informed her that while she might be a veritable she-devil, he was Beelzebub himself. 'With this he took her up by the waist, and, if she made any more words, swore that he would fling her out of the window.' (Mainwaring). Cuzzoni capitulated, and, according to Burney, 'Falsa imagine' 'fixed her reputation as an expressive and pathetic singer'. 'Indeed', continued Burney, 'there is scarce a song in the opera, that did not become a general favourite, either vocally or instrumentally. And the passages in this and the other operas which Handel composed about this time, became the musical language of the nation...'

On 12 January 1723, Cuzzoni made her London début as Teofane, opposite Senesino as Ottone. The combination was electrifying. 'The house was full to overflowing', reported one of the Prince of Wales's Gentlemen of the Bedchamber:

Today is the second performance and there is such a run on it that

The soprano, Francesca Cuzzoni.

tickets are already being sold at 2 and 3 guineas which are ordinarily half a guinea, so that it is like another Mississippi or South Sea Bubble. Over and above that, there exist two factions, the one supporting Hendell, the other Bononcini, the one for Cenesino [Senesino] and the other for Cossuna [Cuzzoni]. They are at much at loggerheads as the Whigs and Tories...

By the middle of the season, London had gone opera-mad. Even the footmen were fighting for places in the theatre galleries. John Gay reported to Jonathan Swift in Dublin:

As for the reigning amusements of the town, it is entirely music... There is nobody allowed to say "I sing", but an eunuch, or an Italian woman. Everybody is grown now as great a judge of music, as they were in your time of poetry, and folks, that could not distinguish one tune from another, now daily dispute about the different styles of Handel, Bononcini and Attilio [Ariosto]. People have now forgot Homer, and Virgil, and Caesar, or at least, they have forgot their ranks; for in London and Westminster, in all polite conversations, Senesino is daily voted to be the greatest man that ever lived.

On 26 March 1723, *Ottone* was revived 'with the Addition of Three new Songs, and an entire new Scene', for Cuzzoni's benefit; 'and a considerable Benefit it was to her indeed, for we hear that some of the Nobility gave her 50 Guineas a Ticket', reported the *London Journal*, who regarded the exorbitant fees demanded by the Italians as 'our Folly'.

Less than two months later, *Flavio* (to a libretto by Haym based on Corneille's famous seventeeth-century drama *Le Cid*) was premièred, with Senesino and Cuzzoni again taking leading rôles. By now deadly rivals, they again starred opposite each other as Caesar and Cleopatra in Handel's masterpiece of politics, revenge and amorous intrigue set in ancient Egypt. *Giulio Cesare* was premièred on 20 February 1724. Burney considered it 'an opera abounding with beauties of various kinds', of which he singled out Cuzzoni's aria 'Troppo crudele siete' ('one of the finest of all Handel's admirable Sicilianas'), the aria 'Priva son; Va tacito' with its horn *obbligato*, and the 'fire and genius' of 'All'lampo dell'armi'. To Burney's list of choice arias might be added Cleopatra's lament 'Piangerò la sorte mia', and her Act Two arias 'V'adoro, pupille' – in which she tries to seduce Caesar, and 'Se pietà di me'.

'The opera is in full swing also, since Hendell's new one, called Jules Cesar [*Giulio Cesare*] – in which Cenesino and Cozzuna shine beyond all criticism – has been put on', reported Monsieur Fabrice, the Prince of Wales's Gentleman of the Bedchamber. 'The house was just as full at the seventh performance as at the

first. In addition to that the squabbles, between the Directors and
the sides that everyone is taking between the singers and the
composers, often provide the public with the most diverting
scenes.' 'The passion for the opera here is getting beyond all
belief. It is true that the music is beautiful and varied', wrote a
French visitor.

91

No.25, Lower Brook Street in a photograph taken in the 1950s.

By the end of the 1724 season, Handel had moved into a newly-built house (now No.25) in Lower Brook Street, near Hanover Square, which was to be his permanent home. During the summer, he rapidly completed his next opera, *Tamerlano*, based on the defeat of the Turkish sultan Bajazet by the Tartar hero Tamburlaine (the subject of Marlowe's famous play); and also gave an organ recital at St Paul's Cathedral, attended by his royal pupils, the Princesses Anne and Caroline. The autumn season – the Academy's sixth – opened with *Tamerlano*, in which several new singers made their débuts. The part of the 'Tyrant Bajazete' was sung by Francesco Borosini, whose tenor voice occasioned much ribald comment among the wits of the day to the effect that 'this Gentleman was never "cut out for a Singer".' The aria 'Bella asteria' in which, according to Burney, Senesino 'greatly distinguished himself', quickly became a popular hit. By mid-January, Handel had finished *Rodelinda*, which was premièred on 13 February 1725, with Cuzzoni (then three months pregnant: she gave birth to a daughter the following August) in the title rôle as a Lombard queen of the early Christian era, distraught at the presumed loss of her husband Bertarido (with whom she is eventually reunited). According to Burney, Cuzzoni 'gained great reputation by the tender and plaintive manner' in which she executed her opening aria, 'Ho perduto il caro sposo'.

By now, Cuzzoni was not only a diva, but a leader of fashion. Burney continues:

The great favour of Cuzzoni received little addition from her personal charms; as Mr Walpole, who perfectly remembers her in the character of Rodelinda, says she was short and squat, with a doughty cross face, but fine complexion; was not a good actress; dressed ill; and was silly and fantastical. And yet on her appearing in this opera, in a brown silk gown, trimmed with silver, with the vulgarity and indecorum of which all the old ladies were much scandalised, the young adopted it as a fashion, so universally, that it seemed a national uniform for youth and beauty.

However, Cuzzoni's monopoly of the London opera stage was shortly to be challenged. Diplomacy was sacrificed to financial gain by the Academy's importation of another diva, guaranteed to inflame still further the wounds inflicted by Cuzzoni's rivalry with Senesino. On 4 September, the *London Journal* announced that 'Signiora Faustina, a famous Italian Lady, is coming over this Winter to rival Signiora Cuzzoni; the Royal Academy of Musick has contracted with her for Two Thousand Five Hundred Pound.' In fact, the Venetian soprano Faustina Bordoni did not arrive in England until May 1726 – and for the same annual

St George's, Hanover Square; Handel's parish church – in a photo taken in the 1950s.

fee (£2,000) as Cuzzoni and Senesino – in time to make her London début in Handel's *Alessandro*. Burney tells us that she:

invented a new kind of singing, by running divisions with a neatness and velocity which astonished all who heard her. She had the art of sustaining a note longer, in the opinion of the public, than any other singer, by taking her breath imperceptibly. Her beats and trills were strong and rapid; her intonation perfect; and her professional perfections were enhanced by a beautiful face, a symmetric figure, though of small stature, and a countenance and gesture on the stage, which indicated an entire intelligence and possession of the several parts she had to represent.

Meanwhile, the Academy's seventh season opened on 30 November 1725 with several revivals, including *Rodelinda*. By now, the winning formula was becoming somewhat stereotyped, subject to the whims of egotistical singers. 'The operas performed in England, fine though they are as regards the music and

Faustina Bordoni; the singer who challenged Cuzzoni's supremacy on the London operatic stage.

FAVSTINA HASSE
Virtuosa di Camera di S Mtà il Re di
Polonia Elettore di Sassonia ノ ? ¿

the voices, are so much hackwork as regards the verses', wrote Giuseppe Riva, Ambassador from the Modenese court, to the historian Muratori. Riva singled out Handel's current librettist, Nicola Haym, for particular censure, for:

adapting – or rather making worse – the old librettos which are already bad enough in their original form... In England they want few recitatives, but thirty arias and one duet at least, distributed over the three acts. The subject-matter must be straightforward, tender, heroic, Roman, Greek, or even Persian...there must be two equal parts in the operas for Cuzzoni and Faustina; Senesino is the chief male character, and his part must be heroic; the other three male parts must proceed by degrees with three arias each, one in each Act. The duet should be at the end of the second Act, and between the two ladies.

On 12 March 1726, Handel's *Scipione* was performed at the Academy. The story concerns the magnanimity of the Roman pro-consul Scipio, who falls in love with his beautiful Carthaginian captive Berenice, but ultimately conquers his passion and returns her to her lover. The famous March which opens Act One was a favourite from the start: according to Burney, it was 'adopted by his Majesty's life-guards, and constantly played on the parade for near forty year.' *Scipione* was the last opera in which Cuzzoni, as Berenice, held undisputed sway on the London stage. According to Burney, the arrival of Faustina a few months later, opened an era in the 'annals of musical contests.'

Alessandro, in which the three *prime donne* appeared together for the first time – Senesino as Alexander the Great, Faustina and Cuzzoni as the two ladies who compete for his love – had 11 performances within a month. Handel expended every effort to provide arias of equal brilliance for both his 'rival queens', including 'Lusinghe più care' and 'Brilla nell'alma' for Faustina; and 'No, più soffrir' and 'L'amor che per te sento' for Cuzzoni. However, according to Burney, 'it seems in general that [Handel] tried to work better for his rival queens, than for the hero of the piece.' Affronted, Senesino retired 'indisposed', and left the country in a fit of pique, bringing the season to a premature close in mid-June. Meanwhile, the delicate problem of how to handle the two great sopranos, each convinced of her own supremacy, posed a dilemma for society hostesses, eager for the prestige of exhibiting both at the same time. Lady Walpole's solution was to remove each by turn 'to a remote part of the house, under the pretence of shewing her some curious china', while the other was singing, under the impression that her rival had quit the field.

Senesino's prolonged sulk delayed the opening of the Academy's autumn season, while, according to Mrs Pendarves, 'Madam Sandoni [Cuzzoni] and the Faustina are not perfectly agreed about their parts'. Meanwhile, John Rich, manager of the Lincoln's Inn Fields Theatre, exploited the Academy's discomfiture by reviving Bononcini's *Camilla*, with a new Prologue referring to the difficulties experienced by the rival house:

> Ye British Fair, vouchsafe us your Applause,
> And smile, propitious, on our English Cause;
> While Senesino you expect in vain,
> And see your Favours treated with Disdain:
> While, 'twixt his Rival Queens, such mutual Hate
> Threatens hourly Ruin to yon tuneful State.
> Permit your Country's Voices to repair,

In some Degree, your Disappointment there:
Here, may that charming Circle Nightly shine;
'Tis Time, when That deserts us, to resign.

Not content with the spectacle of fighting divas – all good for
business – the directors of the Academy decided at the end of
January 1727 to revive internecine warfare among its composers,
by first inviting 'Signior Bononcini to compose an Opera, the
Animosities against that Great Master being worn off', and then
by proposing that Handel and Ariosti should also each compose
a new opera. 'Thus, as this Theatre can boast of the three best
Voices in Europe, and the best Instruments; so the Town will
have the Pleasure of having these three different Stiles of composing.' Meanwhile, Handel's new opera *Admeto*, based on the
Greek legend of Alkestis' death-defying love for her husband, had
opened the season on 31 January, with the mollified Senesino in
the title rôle, Faustina as Alceste, and Cuzzoni as Antigona (a
supernumerary part added in the context of a counterplot).
Admeto enjoyed a longer run – 19 performances – than any other
opera so far. Burney, who noted that its overture owes something
to the style of Lully, drew attention to the 'bold and picturesque
symphony, while Hercules attacks the Furies in order to rescue
Alcestes from their tortures'. Public attention, however, was
focused less on the music than on the two principal protagonists.
The German theorist Quantz, who attended a performance of
Admeto during its first run, neatly summed up the vocal and
physical differences between the 'rival queens':

Cuzzoni had a very agreeable and clear soprano voice; a pure intonation, and a fine shake; her compass extended two octaves from C to c
in alt. Her style of singing was innocent and affecting; her graces did not
seem artificial, from the easy and neat manner in which she executed
them: however, they took possession of the soul of every auditor, by her
tender and touching expression. She had no great rapidity of execution,
in allegros; but there was a roundness and smoothness, which were neat
and pleasing. Yet with all these advantages, it must be owned that she
was rather cold in her action, and her figure was not advantageous for
the stage.
  Faustina had a mezzo-soprano voice, that was less clear than
penetrating. Her compass was only from B flat to G in alt; but after this
time, she extended its limits downwards. She possessed what the
Italians call *un cantar granito*: her execution was articulate and brilliant.
She had a fluent tongue for pronouncing words rapidly and distinctly,
and a flexible throat for divisions, with so beautiful and quick a shake
that she could put it in motion upon short notice, just when she would...
She was doubtless the first who introduced, with success, a swift
repetition of the same tone. She sang adagios with great passion and
expression, but was not equally successful, if such deep sorrow were to

be impressed on the hearer, as might require dragging, sliding, or notes of syncopation, and *tempo rubato*... In her action she was very happy; and as she perfectly possessed that flexibility of muscles and features, which constitutes face-playing, she succeeded equally well in furious, amorous, and tender parts: in short, she was born for singing and for acting.

'What a beautiful mixture it would be, if the excellences of these two angelic beings could be united in a single individual!' sighed the Italian singing teacher Tosi. But according to Quantz, 'The violence of party for the two singers... was so great, that when the admirers of one began to applaud, those of the other were sure to hiss...'

Matters literally came to a head on 6 June 1727, when open fighting broke out between the two factions during a performance of Bononcini's *Astianatte*. According to the *British Journal*:

On Tuesday-Night last, a great Disturbance happened at the Opera, occasioned by the Partisans of the Two Celebrated Rival Ladies, Cuzzoni and Faustina. The Contention at first was only carried on by Hissing on one Side, and Clapping on the other; but proceeded at length to Catcalls, and other great Indecencies: And notwithstanding the Princess Caroline was present, no Regards were of Force to restrain the Rudenesses of the Opponents.

The 'great Indecencies' included calling each other 'bitch' and 'whore', fighting like common fishwives, and pulling each other's head-dresses. The dispute engulfed high society. 'It is not now (as formerly) i.e. are you High Church or Low, Whig or Tory; are you for Court or Country, King George, or the Pretender: but are you for Faustina or Cuzzoni, Handel or Bononcini. There's the Question.'

Just over a fortnight later, the scandal – and the opera season – was cut short by the news of King George's death during a visit to Hanover. On 15 June, the Prince of Wales was proclaimed King George II, and Handel was asked to write the anthems for his coronation on 11 October 1727. Four *Coronation Anthems* – *Let thy Hand be Strengthened, My Heart is Inditing, The King shall Rejoice*, and the ever-popular *Zadok the Priest* – were performed by a choir of 47 male voices drawn mainly from the Chapel Royal, but supplemented by several opera performers, and an orchestra of about 160, 'besides an Organ, which was erected behind the Altar'. Though the orchestra may have come adrift in *My Heart is Inditing* ('The anthems in confusion: all irregular in the music', noted the Archbishop of Canterbury on his service sheet), nevertheless 'both the Musick and the Performers, were the Admiration of all the Audience'.

On the new king's birthday on 30 October, some minuets by Handel were performed at a court ball, and Handel continued to receive an annual salary for teaching George and Caroline's daughters. Earlier in the year, he had taken the precaution of applying for naturalisation as a British subject, which had been granted by Act of Parliament on 20 February.

Meanwhile, the ninth opera season opened on 30 September 1727 with a revival of *Admeto*. The Academy was in deep financial trouble: having employed the best singers in Europe at prices far higher than it could afford, it was forced to 'call' on its weary subscribers – many of whom were themselves in debt – for the nineteenth time. Handel dutifully provided no less than three new operas – *Riccardo Primo* (based, in patriotic homage to the new king, on the life of a previous English monarch); *Siroe* (whose première on 17 February 1728 was attended by the royal family); and *Tolomeo, rè di Egitto* (30 April). Though all three starred Senesino, Cuzzoni and Faustina, the Academy was tottering towards collapse. 'I doubt operas will not survive longer than this winter, they are now at their last gasp; the subscription is expired and nobody will renew it', wrote Mrs Pendarves in November 1727. 'The directors are always squabbling, and they have so many divisions among themselves that I wonder they have not broke up before; Senesino goes away next winter, and I believe Faustina, so you see harmony is almost out of fashion.' The *coup de grâce* was delivered at the end of January 1728, when, during the rehearsals of *Siroe*, John Gay's famous *Beggar's Opera* was produced at the Lincoln's Inn Fields Theatre. 'Yesterday I was at the rehearsal of the new opera composed by Handel', wrote Mrs Pendarves. 'I like it extremely, but the taste of the town is so depraved, that nothing will be approved of but the burlesque. The Beggar's Opera entirely triumphs over the Italian one...' Gay's vernacular satire, with music arranged by Pepusch not only from popular ballads, but also from airs pillaged from various composers – including Handel's march from *Rinaldo* – did indeed take the town by storm. *The Beggar's Opera* itself quickly spawned parodies lampooning its rivals, such as *Polly Peachum* (sung to the tune 'Of all the Girls that are so Smart'):

> Of all the Belles that tread the Stage
> There's none like pretty *Polly*,
> And all the Musick of the Age,
> Except her Voice, is Folly.
>
> Compar'd with her, how flat appears
> *Cuzzoni* or *Faustina*?
> And when she sings, I shut my Ears
> To warbling *Senesino*.

King George II in a portrait by Thomas Hudson.

The Beggar's Opera. The prison scene painted by Gilbert Newton.

Mainwaring attributed the Academy's troubles largely to the continuing wrangles between Handel and the intransigent and costly 'Canary-birds'.

SENESINO...began to feel his strength and importance. He felt them so much, that what he had hitherto regarded as legal government, now appeared to him in the light of downright tyranny. Handel, perceiving that he was grown less tractable and obsequious, resolved to subdue these Italian humours, not by lenitives, but sharp corrosives. To manage him he disdained; to control him with a high-hand, he in vain attempted. The one was perfectly refractory; the other was equally outrageous. In short, matters had proceeded so far, that there were no hopes of an accommodation... Whatever they were, the Nobility would not consent to his design of parting with SENESINO, and Handel was determined to have no further concerns with him. FAUSTINA and CUZZONI, as if seized with the contagion of discord, started questions of superiority, and urged their respective claims to it with an eagerness and acrimony, which occasioned a total dis-union betwixt them.

Although *Siroe*, the story of a Persian prince's attempt to regain the rightful throne of which his father had tried to deprive him,

100

A 'stage medley' from
The Beggar's Opera.

had a respectable run of 18 performances, *Tolomeo* – another story of royal rivalry (this time for the throne of Egypt)– had only seven. By the end of March, the *London Journal* was remarking on the 'Neglect into which the Italian Operas are at present fallen; so I cannot but think it a very extraordinary Instance of the fickle and inconstant Temper of the English Nation'. On 5 June, the Academy called a meeting of its subscribers to consider ways of recovering and discharging its debts, and to prepare for liquidation by disposing of its assets; while the season itself came to an abrupt end with the indisposition of Faustina. 'And thus the Academy, after it had continued in the most flourishing state for upwards of nine years, was at once dissolved.' (Mainwaring).

Chapter 8

From Opera to Oratorio

As a salaried employee, Handel seems to have suffered no personal financial loss on the collapse of the Academy. Over the summer of 1728, he bought over £1,000 worth of South Sea annuities, which he sold again six months later, presumably to finance an ambitious venture. In mid-January 1729, the directors of the Academy granted Heidegger and Handel a lease of the King's Theatre, 'to carry on operas without disturbance for 5 years and to lend them for that time all our scenes, machines, clothes, instruments, furniture, etc.' Heidegger was to receive £2,200 'with which to provide the theatre, the scenery and the costumes', while Handel would be paid £1,000 for composing and organising the music. A realistic budget for the cast was set at £4,000 – enough to hire two principals at £1,000 each, and the rest divided among the *comprimarii*. Meanwhile, both partners – thoroughly tired of the incessant squabbling between the Academy's former principal singers (Handel in particular wanted the opportunity of writing new works for different performers) – decided to scour the Continent for new soloists. After a fruitless quest, Heidegger returned with the bright idea of re-engaging the 'two ladies', though the question of Senesino's reinstatement – to which Handel remained implacably opposed – presented diplomatic problems. According to Mainwaring:

[Handel] remained inflexible in his resolution to punish Senesino for refusing him that submission, which he had been used to receive, and which he thought he had a right to demand: but a little pliability would have saved him abundance of trouble. The vacancy made by the removal of such a Singer was not easily supplied. The umbrage which [Handel] had given to many of the Nobility, by his implacable resentments against a person whose talents they so much admired, was likely to create him a dangerous opposition. For, tho' he continued at the Hay-market, yet, in the heat of these animosities, a great part of his audience would melt away.

The King's Theatre, Haymarket, from an original drawing by William Capon.

In early February 1729, Handel himself left on a recruitment drive. Both Senesino and Faustina were singing in Venice, Handel's first stop; while in Rome he, like Heidegger, was much impressed by the great Italian castrato Farinelli, with whom he opened negotiations. Some months later, the malicious Rolli reported to Senesino that 'The Man [Handel] returned from his travels very full of Farinello [sic] and extremely loud in his praises'; but Senesino refused to rise to the bait. In June, Handel paid a brief visit to Halle, where he saw his mother – who died the following year – for the last time. At the end of the month, he returned to London with a new company, including the Italian sopranos Anna Strada and Margherita Merighi, the mezzo Francesca Bertolli, and his old school-fellow from Hamburg, the German bass J.G. Riemschneider. Only one singer, the celebrated male soprano Antonio Bernacchi (at £1,200, the highest-paid), had previously sung in London. Handel presented his troupe at Court for a 'private Performance before their Majesties at Kensington; when the Harpsichord was played on by Mr Handell, and their Performances were much approved.'

The new Academy's first season opened on 2 December 1729 with *Lotario*, a historical romance based on the characters of Otto I, King of Germany and later Holy Roman Emperor, and his wife Adelaide. It ran for ten performances, without outstanding success. 'Everyone considers it a very bad opera', wrote Rolli, to a friend.

In person and voice [Bernacchi] does not please as much as Senesino, but his great reputation as an artist silences those who cannot find it in them to applaud him. The truth is that he has only one aria in which he can shine… Strada pleases mightily… The truth is that she has a penetrating thread of a soprano voice which delights the ear, but oh, how far removed from Cuzzona! Fabri is a great success… There is a certain Bertolli, a Roman girl, who plays men's parts. Oh!… if you could only see her perspiring under her helmet – I am sure you would fall in love with her… She is a pretty one! There is also a bass from Hamburg whose voice is more of a natural contralto than a bass. He sings sweetly in his throat and nose, pronounces Italian in the Teutonic manner, acts like a sucking pig, and looks more like a *valet* than anything else… They are putting on *Giulio Cesare* because the audiences are falling away fast. I think the storm is about to break on the head of our proud *Orso* [Bear = Handel]. Not all beans are for market, especially beans so badly cooked as this first basketful.

'The opera is too good for the vile taste of this town… We are to have some old opera revived, which I am sorry for, it will put people upon making comparisons between these singers and those that performed before, which will be a disadvantage among the ill-judging multitude. The present opera is disliked because it is much too studied, and they love nothing but minuets and ballads', wrote Mrs Pendarves. Handel tried to retrieve the situation with *Partenope*, the story of a queen and her three suitors. Premièred on 24 February 1730, it had seven performances which failed to draw full houses.

His first solo season had been an unmitigated disaster. Realising that the problem lay with his cast, Handel was forced to swallow his pride, and re-engage Senesino in place of Bernacchi, at a salary of 1,400 guineas. With the arrogant castrato restored to his rightful place, the new company's second season opened on 3 November 1730 with a revival of *Scipione*, in the presence of the King and Queen. 'Senesino being return'd charm'd much', reported the *Opera Register*. Three months later, *Poro*, based on a love triangle – concocted by Metastasio – between Alexander the Great, Porus (king of an Indian region which Alexander has conquered), and the object of their joint desire, Porus's fellow-monarch Queen Cleofide, had its première on 2 February 1731.

With Senesino in the title rôle and Strada as Cleofide, it achieved a reasonable success, especially the aria 'Son confusa pastorella', which became known as the 'favourite hornpipe' or 'the bagpipe song'. (According to Burney, it 'was long in high favour, not only with singers, but performers upon the German-flute'.) The scores of both *Partenope* and *Poro* were engraved by the firm of John Walsh, who for years had been issuing the 'favourite songs' from Handel's works in a variety of best-selling formats, without the composer's permission. From then onwards, Handel adopted the enterprising Walsh as his 'official' publisher.

The season continued with revivals of *Rinaldo* and *Rodelinda*; while in March 1731, 'at the Desire of several Persons of Quality', *Acis and Galatea* (Handel's Cannons pastorale) was performed for the first time in public at the rival Lincoln's Inn Fields Theatre, with an English cast, including the famous bass Richard Leveridge as Polyphemus. It is not known whether Handel sanctioned the performance.

At the King's Theatre, the 1731/2 season opened on 13 November with revivals of *Tamerlano*, *Poro* and *Admeto*, which marked the London début of the Italian bass Antonio Montagnana, whose powerful voice extended over two octaves. Then, in January 1732, Handel and Heidegger suffered their most serious set-back to date, with the utter failure of *Ezio* (a tale of love and jealousy set in the last decades of the Roman Empire). Even with Senesino in the title rôle, and Montagnana as his loyal friend Varus, *Ezio* failed to catch on, and had only five performances. The *Opera Register* for that month, reported '*Ezio* – a New Opera, Clothes & all ye Scenes New – but did not draw much Company'. To repair the damage, the old warhorse *Giulio Cesare* was revived once more, followed by another new opera, *Sosarme, rè di Media*, which enjoyed 11 performances '& was for many Nights much crowded to some people's admiration'. Viscount Percival thought it 'one of the best I ever heard'. The plot deals with a family feud in which a son is in open rebellion against his father, the king. The rift is widened by the evil machinations of the king's chief minister, but eventually the royal family, inspired by the noble example of the king's future son-in-law, Sosarme, effects a reconciliation between father and son. Audiences of the time no doubt noticed a close parallel between events in *Sosarme* and the open antagonism between their own king, George II, and his eldest son, Frederick, Prince of Wales. Learning from previous errors of judgment, Handel made heavy cuts to the recitatives in *Sosarme*, thereby sacrificing dramatic continuity to the limited concentration-span of his audiences.

In general, the public was growing weary of Italian opera, and sought fresh novelty to tempt their jaded palates. On 23 February

1732, Viscount Percival 'went to the Music Club, where the King's Chapel boys acted the *History of Hester*, writ by Pope and composed by Hendel. This oratorio or religious opera is exceeding fine, and the company were highly pleased, some of the parts being well performed.'

At that time, the Philharmonic Society (also known as the 'Society for Gentlemen Performers of Music', or simply as the 'Music Club') met privately to give amateur performances on Wednesday evenings at the Crown and Anchor Tavern in the Strand. The Duke of Chandos had recently joined, and it was doubtless he who suggested that Handel's Cannons oratorio should be resurrected. According to the libretto:

Mr Bernard Yates [Gates], Master of the Children of the Chapel Royal, together with a number of voices from the Choirs of the Chapel Royal and Westminster, join'd in Chorus's after the manner of the Ancients, being placed between the stage and the Orchestra; and the Instrumental parts (two or three particular instruments, necessary on the Occasion Excepted) were perform'd by the members of the Philharmonic Society consisting only of Gentlemen.

Impresarios were quick to sense a sea-change. By 19 April, an unauthorised public performance of *Esther* (probably instigated

Handel directing an oratorio, from a rare print in the British Museum.

by John Rich) had been announced in the Great Room [Hickford's Room] in York Buildings: while Handel, apparently at the personal request of his pupil Princess Anne, announced a similar performance at the King's Theatre on 2 May, adding, 'Formerly composed by Mr Handel, and revised by him, with several Additions, and to be performed by a great number of the best Voices and Instruments'. Handel also advised that 'There will be no Action on the Stage [apparently the result of a prohibition by the Bishop of London], but the House will be fitted up in a decent Manner, for the Audience. The Musick to be disposed after the Manner of the Coronation Service.' With Senesino as Ahasuerus, Montagnana as Haman, and Strada as Esther, supported by three English singers, *Esther* was a triumph. Viscount Percival reported, 'In the evening I went to Hendel's oratorio. The Royal Family was there, and the house crowded.' The court seems to have attended at least three performances, and the *London Magazine* reported that the oratorio drew 'vast Applause'.

'The applause with which it was received, suggested to Mr Handel the thought of exhibiting that species of composition at Covent Garden Theatre', wrote Hawkins, and *Esther*'s success did not pass unnoticed by the wits of the day:

> Without Italian, or without an ear,
> To Bononcini's musick I adhere...
> Bagpipes for men, shrill *German-flutes* for boys,
> I'm *English*-born, and love a grumbling noise.
> The Stage should yield the solemn Organ's note,
> And Scripture tremble in the Eunuch's throat.
> Let *Senesino* sing, what David writ,
> And *Hallelujahs* charm the pious pit.
> Eager in throngs the town to *Hester* came,
> And *Oratorio* was a lucky name.
> Thou, *Heideggre*! [sic] the English taste has found,
> And rul'st the mob with quality of sound.
> In *Lent*, if Masquerades displease the town,
> Call'em *Ridotto's*, and they still go down:
> Go on, Prime *Phyz*! to please the British nation,
> Call thy next *Masquerade* a *Convocation*.

Apart from the Lincoln's Inn Fields Theatre company, the King's Theatre had a new and potentially more dangerous rival just across the road – the New Theatre in the Haymarket (opened in 1720), where, since 13 March 1732, Thomas Arne senior had been producing 'English Operas'. On 2 May, the *Daily Post* announced that the 'English Opera will very shortly perform a celebrated Pastoral Opera call'd ACIS and GALATEA, compos'd by Mr Handel'. Handel's reaction to this naked act of defiance was to organise his own counter-production of *Acis*. 'There will be no Action on the Stage', advised the *Daily Courant*, 'but the Scene will represent, in a Picturesque Manner, a rural Prospect, with Rocks, Groves, Fountains and Grotto's; amongst which will be disposed a Chorus of Nymphs and Shepherds, Habits, and every other Decoration suited to the Subject'. Handel's 'revised' version was a bilingual, three-act mish-mash of both his *Acis* settings, with English and Italian airs and choruses drawn from each. The Italian singers, including Senesino as Acis, Strada as Galatea and Montagnana as Polyphemus, sang in Italian, and the two English singers in their native tongue. Despite this absurdity, Viscount Percival thought it a 'fine masque'.

The success of *Acis* and *Esther* lay in the fact that English audiences wanted to hear their own language on stage. An anonymous satirical pamphlet in epistolary form (*See and Seem Blind: Or, A Critical Dissertation of the Publick Diversions &c*) summed up the public mood:

…I left the *Italian* Opera, the House was so thin, and cross'd over the way to the *English* one, which was so full I was forc'd to croud in upon the Stage…

This alarm'd *H-l*, and out he brings an *Oratorio*, or Religious *Farce*, for the duce take me if I can make any other Construction of the Word, but he has made a very good *Farce* of it, and put near £4,000 in his Pocket… This being a new Thing set the whole World a Madding; Han't you be at the *Oratorio*, says one? Oh! If you don't see the *Oratorio* you see nothing, says t'other; so away goes I to the *Oratorio*, where I saw indeed the finest Assembly of People I ever beheld in my Life, but, to my great Surprize, found this Sacred *Drama* a mere Consort, no Scenary, Dress, or Action, so necessary to a *Drama*… Strada gave us a *Halleluiah* of Half an Hour long; *Senesino* and *Bertolli* made rare work with the *English* Tongue you would have sworn it had been *Welch*; I would have wish'd it *Italian*, that they might have sung with more ease to themselves, since, but for the name of *English*, it might as well have been *Hebrew*… Were they indeed to make a regular *Drama* of a good Scripture Story, and perform'd it with proper Decorations, which may be done with as much Preverence in proper Habits, as in their own common Apparel…then should I change my Mind, then would the Stage appear in its full Lustre, and Musick Answer its original Design.

In December 1732, Handel's old colleague Aaron Hill pleaded with him to:

let us owe to your inimitable genius, the establishment of *musick*, upon a foundation of good poetry; where the excellence of the *sound* should be no longer dishonour'd, by the poorness of the *sense* it is chain'd to.

My meaning is, that you would be resolute enough, to deliver us from our *Italian bondage*; and demonstrate, that *English* is soft enough for

Opera, when compos'd by poets, who know how to distinguish the *sweetness* of our tongue, from the *strength* of it, where the last is less necessary... I am sure, a species of dramatic Opera might be invented that, by reconciling reason and dignity, would charm the *ear*, and hold fast the *heart*, together.

Handel remained unmoved. Despite the success of *Acis* and *Esther*, his faith for the time being still lay with Italian opera. In the autumn of 1732, he engaged a new Italian singer, the mezzo-soprano Celeste Gismondi, known as '*La Celestina*'. She made her début on 4 November in a *pasticcio* based on Leo's *Catone in Utica*, which Lord Hervey, mistaking the music for Handel's, found 'long, dull and consequently tiresome'. Celestina, however, 'seemed to take mightily'. Rumours abounded that Handel's 'genius was exhausted': a revival of *Alessandro* later in November drew only a 'thin House' at its second performance; but, after a similarly disappointing revival of *Tolomeo*, Handel struck back at his critics with a new opera. *Orlando*, premièred on 27 January 1733, is one of his finest achievements. Based on an episode from Ariosto's epic *Orlando furioso* (which also supplied the subject of Lully's 1685 masterpiece *Roland*), *Orlando* is a study in the Baroque concept of *gloire*: the triumph of a hero's pursuit of glory over the snares of love. Orlando's unrequited love for the faithless Angelica, Queen of Cathay, leads him to temporary insanity, from which he is rescued by the magician Zoroastre. Burney comments on the 'wild grandeur' of the opening night scene, which depicted Zoroastre (sung by Montagnana) meditating on the motions of the heavenly bodies; and on the last scene in Act Two: 'The whole last scene of this act, which paints the madness of Orlando, in accompanied recitatives and airs in various measures, is admirable. Handel has endeavoured to describe the hero's perturbation of intellect by fragments of symphony in 5/8, a division of time which can only be borne in such a situation.'

Although *Orlando* had 11 performances, and was described by the *Opera Register* as 'extraordinary fine & magnificent', Handel's company was in serious trouble. Many of his former noble supporters, alarmed by the apparent decline of Italian opera, blamed Handel, particularly for his continuing feud with Senesino. In January 1733, the Earl of Delaware wrote to the Duke of Richmond: 'There is a Spirit got up against the Dominion of Mr Handel, a subscription carry'd on, and Directors chosen, who have contracted with Senesino, and have sent for Cuzzoni and Farinelli... The General Court gave power to contract with any Singer Except Strada, so that it is Thought Handel must fling up, which the Poor Count [Heidegger] will not be sorry for... Porpora is also sent for...' This was the first intimation that a rival company was about to be set up, backed by many erstwhile subscribers to the Handel-Heidegger régime. Sensing danger, Handel responded with another oratorio, *Deborah*, which was performed at the King's Theatre on 17 March. 'It was very magnificent, near a hundred performers, among whom about twenty-five singers', reported Viscount Percival. But for once, Handel's sound business sense deserted him, resulting in a catastrophic error of judgment which would haunt him for years. He took the opportunity of doubling the subscription ticket prices to a guinea for the first night, a highly unpopular move which happened to coincide with the introduction of an equally loathed Parliamentary measure – Prime Minister Robert Walpole's Tobacco Excise Bill. Handel and Walpole found themselves bracketed together by the gutter press as

Sir Robert Walpole painted by Jean-Baptiste van Loo.

greedy and unscrupulous manipulators: an epigram circulating at the time ran:

A *Dialogue* between two *Projectors*

Quoth W[alpole] to H[andel] shall we two agree,
And join in a Scheme of Excise. H. *Caro sì.*
Of what Use is your Sheep if your Shepherd can't shear him?
At the Hay-Market I, you at We[stminst]er? W. *Hear him.*
Call'd to Order the Seconds appear'd in their Place,
One fam'd for his Morals, and one for his Face;
In half they succeeded, in half they were crost;
The *Tobacco* was sav'd, but poor *Deborah* lost.

Both hastily backed down, but *Deborah*, based on the story of Deborah, Jael and Barak as recounted in Chapter 4 of *Judges*, had only five further performances before the King's Theatre closed for refurbishment. Shortly afterwards, Handel was scurrilously attacked in the press by Rolli, who accused him of dictatorial arrogance in his treatment of singers, and of extortion, by diverting all the proceeds from the oratorios 'for his own benefit'. Rolli concluded his libellous attack by hinting that Handel was mentally deranged:

This Accident [the desertion of his audiences] they say, has thrown Him into a *deep Melancholy*, interrupted sometimes by *raving fits*; in which he fancies he sees ten thousand *Opera* Devils coming to tear Him to Pieces; then He breaks out into frantick, incoherent Speeches; muttering *sturdy Beggars*, *Assassination*, &c... It is much question'd whether he will recover...

In the teeth of mounting public criticism of his treatment of their darling, Handel finally dismissed Senesino at the end of May. The press remarked that 'the World seems greatly ASTONISH'D at so unexpected an Event; and that all true Lovers of Musick GRIEVE to see so fine a Singer dismissed, in so critical a Conjuncture.' At the close of the season, Handel's entire Italian cast, with the exception of Anna Strada, deserted him to join the new Opera of the Nobility, which was then preparing to open in the autumn under the patronage of the Prince of Wales.

Meanwhile, Handel had been invited to Oxford by Dr William Holmes, Vice-Chancellor of the University, ostensibly 'in order to take his Degree in Musick; a Favour that University intends to compliment him with, at the ensuing Publick Act [the degree-giving ceremony].' Pleading that he was 'too overwhelmingly busy', Handel declined the offer of an honorary degree, but took

Eighteenth-century view of Oxford.

Two Oxford scenes showing Magdalen College and the Sheldonian Theatre where several of Handel's oratorios were performed.

his depleted company – now consisting mainly of English singers – to Oxford to perform *Esther, Deborah, Acis* and a new oratorio – *Athaliah* – in the Sheldonian Theatre, newly 'fitted up' for the occasion. Handel was also allowed to give benefit performances within the University itself, in order to defray some of his expenses. 'The Vice-Chancellour is much blamed for it', grumbled a discontented don, who would almost have preferred to see the sacred precincts defiled by common actors than 'Handel and (his lowsy Crew) a great number of forreign fidlers'. Oxford itself was crowded with visitors for the occasion; and Handel's performances were packed out. At the première of *Athaliah* on 10 July, contemporary reports put the audience at 3,700. The *Norwich Gazette* reported that 'towards Evening an oratorio of Mr Handell's called Arthur [sic] was performed by about 70 Voices and Instruments of Musick, and was the grandest ever heard at Oxford. It is computed that the Tickets which were only 5s each amounted to £700.' By 21 July, it was rumoured that

Handel had made some £2,000 out of his 'Musick at Oxford', which included, in addition to the oratorios and *Acis*, concerts, performances at St Mary's Church of the *Utrecht Te Deum* and *Jubilate* and two Coronation anthems during the five-day ceremony.

On 30 October 1733, the King's birthday, Handel launched his next opera season two months ahead of his rivals with two *pasticcios*, *Semiramide riconosciuto*, and *Cajo Fabricio*. Neither was a success. Although the entire royal family attended a subsequent revival of *Ottone* in November, the *beau monde* eagerly awaited the début of the Opera of the Nobility, with its illustrious cast of stars including Senesino and Montagnana (Cuzzoni was to join them in April). After a rehearsal on Christmas Eve at the Prince of Wales's house in the Royal Gardens at Pall Mall, attended by a 'great Concourse of the Nobility and Quality of both Sexes', the new company opened on 29 December 1733 at the Theatre Royal in Lincoln's Inn Fields with Porpora's *Arianna in Nasso*, to a text by the treacherous Rolli. A month later, Handel responded with his own setting of the Ariadne legend, *Arianna in Creta*, with Strada as Arianna and Giovanni Carestini – the replacement for Senesino – as Teseo. 'Ariadne in Crete a new Opera & very good & perform'd very often – Sigr Carestino sung surprisingly well: a new Eunuch – many times perform'd', reported the *Opera Register*. Carestini, the 'new Eunuch', possessed (according to Burney), 'the fullest, finest, and deepest counter-tenor that has perhaps ever been heard... [his] person was tall, beautiful, and majestic. He was a very animated and intelligent actor, and having a considerable portion of enthusiasm in his composition, with a lively and inventive imagination, he rendered everything he sung interesting by good taste, energy, and judicious embellishments.' Enhanced by Carestini's presence, Handel's *Arianna* had a respectable run of 17 performances, and was attended twice by the Court – including the renegade Prince of Wales.

In March 1734, Handel was invited to write a serenata and a wedding anthem for the marriage of his favourite pupil, Anne, 'the flower of princesses'. The performance of *Il Parnasso in festa*, attended by the royal family and Anne's bridegroom, the Prince of Orange, took place at the King's Theatre on 13 March against a single backdrop representing 'Mount Parnassus, on which sit Apollo and the Muses, assisted with other proper Characters, emblematically dress'd, the whole Appearance being extreamly magnificent. The Musick is no less entertaining, being contriv'd with so great a Variety, that all Sorts of Musick are properly introduc'd in single Songs, Duetto's, &c intermix'd with Chorus's, some what in the Style of Oratorio's.' (In fact, the music was largely drawn from *Athaliah*, which had not been

114

performed in London.) The following day, Handel's wedding anthem *This is the Day* was performed 'by a great number of voices and instruments' at the marriage service held at the Queen's Chapel in St James's Palace.

But despite continuing royal patronage, Handel had cause for concern. Both his company and the Opera of the Nobility were playing to thin houses. 'I go tonight to…*Sosarmes*, an opera of Mr Handel's, a charming one, and yet I dare say it will be almost empty!' wrote Mrs Pendarves. ''Tis vexatious to have *such music* neglected.' A revival of his 1712 opera *Il pastor fido*, augmented by new music, concluded Handel's least successful season to date. His contract expired on 6 July, and Heidegger promptly let the King's Theatre to the Opera of the Nobility. Though false rumours abounded that Handel would be 'obliged to leave London and return to his native land', he made an agreement with John Rich to put on operas at Rich's theatre in Covent Garden, and retired to the spa at Tunbridge Wells to mull over the situation. The season had been an utter failure, both artistically and financially, and in June he had been obliged to withdraw £1,300 from his own bank account to offset his loss. In October 1734, King George, probably as a result of pressure from his eldest daughter, ordered that the royal annual subscription of £1,000 should be paid direct to the distressed composer, rather than to the opera company.

By this time, the rivalry between the two factions had split London society from top to bottom, and was causing bitter dissension among the Royal Family. According to Lord Hervey, the Prince of Wales disapproved so strongly of his sister's support for Handel that:

in the beginning of his enmity to his sister, [he] set himself at the head of the other opera to irritate her… The King and Queen were as much in earnest upon this subject as their son and daughter though they had the prudence to…endeavour to disguise it… They were both Handelists, and sat freezing constantly at his empty Haymarket Opera, while the Prince with all the chief of nobility went as constantly to that of Lincoln's Inn Fields.

Apparently undeterred by its own losses, the Opera of the Nobility prepared its next season, at ever-increasing expense. 'We hear that both Operas (occasion'd by their dividing) are at a vast expence to entertain the Nobility and Gentry for the ensuing Season; the Opera House in the Haymarket are reckon'd to stand near £12,000 and Mr Handell at near £9,000 for the season', remarked the *Ipswich Gazette* at the beginning of November. The Nobility opened first with Hasse's *Artaserse*, featuring the Italian castrato Farinelli, whom Handel had tried

Italian castrato Farinelli, hired at extortionate cost to sing for the Opera of the Nobility.

and failed to attract to England. Both the ageing Senesino and Carestini realised that neither could compete with the greatest singer of his day, blessed with 'a voice of uncommon power, sweetness, extent, and agility'. Rolli wrote that 'Farinello was a revelation to me, for I realised that till then I had only heard a small part of what human song can achieve, whereas I now conceive I have heard all there is to hear'; while according to Burney, 'Senesino had the part of a furious tyrant, and Farinelli that of an unfortunate hero in chains; but in the course of the first air, the captive so softened the heart of the tyrant, that Senesino, forgetting his stage-character, ran to Farinelli and embraced him in his own.' Deprived of the best singers and players, Handel responded on 9 November 1734 with a revival of *Il pastor fido*, in

116

an expanded and revised version. It featured the 'extreme fine English Voice' of the tenor John Beard, formerly of the Chapel Royal, and from then onwards a mainstay of Handel's company. But Handel's star attraction was the virtuoso French dancer Marie Sallé. A pioneering exponent of the expressive, naturalistic style of dance later advocated by Noverre, this eighteenth-century Isadora Duncan had created a sensation at Drury Lane earlier in the year when Rich had engaged her for the ballet *Pygmalion*. In contrast to the formal costumes and stylised gestures to which Baroque opera audiences were accustomed, Sallé dared to appear 'without a pannier, skirt or bodice, and with her hair down; she did not wear a single ornament on her head. Apart from her corset and petticoat, she wore only a simple muslin robe, draped round her after the fashion of a Greek statue'. To display Sallé's abilities to best effect, Handel prefaced *Il pastor fido* with 'a new Dramatick Entertainment of Musick' – the unique one-act, French-style opera-ballet *Terpsicore*. She also appeared in the ensuing revival of *Arianna*, and in the *pasticcio-*

Marie Sallé in an engraving after Lancret.

Interior of the Old Theatre Royal, Drury Lane, viewed from the stage.

opera *Oreste* (for which Handel provided three new arias), produced on 18 December.

Meanwhile, with breathtaking audacity, the Haymarket Theatre staged Handel's own *Ottone*, with Farinelli as Adelberto. 'I don't pity Handell in the least, for I hope this mortification will make him a human creature; for I am sure before he was no better than a brute, when he could treat civilized people with so much brutality as I know he has done', wrote an unknown correspondent to Catherine Collingwood. Handel immediately responded with a new work, *Ariodante*, a tale of love, jealousy and thwarted ambition set in Scotland in Arthurian times, but without the heroic or magical elements which had cluttered many of his previous plots. Premièred on 8 January 1735, *Ariodante* featured – besides extensive dance music for Marie Sallé – Carestini in the title rôle, the German bass Gustavus Waltz (who apparently doubled as Handel's cook), as the King of Scotland, Strada as his daughter Ginevra, and a new soprano, Cecilia Young (who later married the composer Thomas Arne) as Dalinda, Ginevra's confidante. According to Burney, 'Waltz had but little voice, and his manner was coarse and unpleasant'; and despite an effective 'moonlight scene' at the beginning of Act Two, Burney detected

118

a lack of variety in the libretto, which resulted in 'fewer capital and captivating airs than some of [Handel's] previous dramas'. *Ariodante* achieved ten performances, in competition with Porpora's *Polifemo* at the Haymarket. 'After which', as Burney remarked, 'as Handel's capital singers were inferior in number and renown to those of his rival, he very wisely discontinued the performance of operas for a considerable time, and rested his fame and fortune on his choral strength in the composition of oratorios...'

Esther, *Deborah* and *Athaliah* were all revived during the spring of 1735, with an additional novelty: Handel began to play his own organ concertos in the intervals, a practice he continued to the end of his life, even after he had lost his sight. Mrs Pendarves considered Handel's performances in *Esther* 'the finest things I ever heard in my life'.

Even so, the theatre remained half-empty, while according to the press, the Opera of the Nobility flourished due to the success of Farinelli, who 'surpasses every thing we have hitherto heard'. '*Handel*, whose excellent Compositions have often pleased our Ears, and touched our Hearts, has this Winter sometimes performed to an almost empty Pitt', wrote an anonymous observer in *The Old Whig*. 'He has lately reviv'd his fine *Oratorio* of *Esther*, in which he has introduced two Concerto's on the Organ that are inimitable. But so strong is the Disgust taken against him, that even this has been far from bringing him crowded Audiences; tho' there were no other publick Entertainments on those Evenings. His Loss is computed for these two Seasons at a great Sum'.

In April, Handel made another attempt to regain his former supremacy on the operatic stage with *Alcina*, based on another episode from *Orlando furioso*. Like Circe, Alcina is a sorceress who lives on an enchanted island, turning her discarded lovers into animals or inanimate objects before she herself is finally destroyed by her consuming passion for the hero Ruggiero. With Strada in the title rôle, *Alcina*'s première on 16 April was attended by the royal family: it had a record run of 18 performances. Mrs Pendarves thought it 'the best [Handel] ever made...'tis so fine I have not words to describe it. Strada has a whole scene of charming recitative – there are a thousand beauties. Whilst Mr Handel was playing his part [on the harpsichord] I could not help thinking him a necromancer in the midst of his own enchantments.' *Alcina*, according to Burney, was 'an opera with which Handel seems to have vanquished his opponents, and to have kept the field near a month longer than his rival Porpora was able to make head against him ...few of his productions have been more frequently performed, or more generally and deservedly admired than this opera.' Burney points out that while some attributed *Alcina*'s unexpected success to Handel's adoption of the fashionable galant style of Vinci, Porpora and Hasse, 'the best and most favourite airs of the opera were certainly composed by Handel in his own manner, without leaning to that of others'. One of the opera's best arias, 'Verdi prati', caused yet another irreconcilable rift between Handel and his principal male singer: Carestini initially refused to sing it, until 'a typical Handelian rejoinder' persuaded him to reconsider his decision. Like Senesino before him, Carestini then decided that he could take no more of Handel's dictatorial treatment: at the close of the season he left for Italy, and never sang for Handel again. The final performance of *Alcina* also marked Marie Sallé's exit – hissed off the stage for offending English propriety. She 'cast herself for the rôle of Cupid and took upon herself to dance it in male attire. This, it is said, suits her very ill and was apparently the cause of her disgrace', reported her countryman the Abbé Prevost. Her departure drew some ribald sallies from the English press:

> The French us English oft deride
> And for our unpoliteness chide:
> Mam Sallé too (late come from France)
> Says we can neither dress nor dance,
> Yet she, as t'is agreed by most,
> Dresses and dances at our cost.
> She from experience draws her rules,
> And Justly Calls the English fools.
> For such they are, since none but such
> For foreign Tilts would pay so much.

Alcina's success could not compensate for the failure of the season as a whole. Handel lost around £9,000; but despite the continuing public adoration of Farinelli, his rivals had fared even worse. In October, the *General Evening Post* reported that 'Mr Handell will perform Oratorios and have Concerts of Musick, this Winter, at Covent-Garden Theatre'; while the Opera of the Nobility unwisely persisted with opera in the face of public apathy.

On 19 February 1736, Handel's setting of *Alexander's Feast*, an ode originally composed by Jeremiah Clarke in 1697 for the annual St Cecilia celebrations at Stationers' Hall, was performed at the Theatre Royal in Covent Garden, with one Italian (Strada) and three English singers. 'Never was upon any like Occasion so numerous and splendid an Audience at any Theatre in London, there being at least 1,300 Persons present; and it is judg'd that the Receipt of the House could not amount to less than £450. It met with general Applause, tho' attended with the Inconvenience of having the Performers plac'd at too great a distance from the Audience, which we hear will be rectified the next Time of Performance', reported the *London Daily Post*.

Alexander's Feast, Dryden's account of a celebration held by Alexander the Great after defeating Darius of Persia (a text which offered many colourful opportunities to illuminate the power of music in the service of valour), had five performances. By April, however, Handel had once more turned his attention to opera. The Prince of Wales was about to marry Augusta, Princess of Saxe-Gotha, and Handel – as a gesture of reconciliation – was asked to arrange an opera season for the entertainment of the royal couple. On her arrival from Germany, Augusta was received at Greenwich, where the Prince visited her the day before the wedding, and the couple passed the evening in a barge on the water, serenaded by music (quite possibly the same *Water Music* with which Handel had entertained the Prince's grand-father). Handel was also asked to supply an anthem (*Sing unto God*) for the marriage service, which took place in the Chapel Royal in St James's Palace on 27 April, earlier than anticipated. 'There was a prodigious crowd... The chapel was finely adorned with tapestry, velvet and gold lace... Over the altar was placed the

A view from One Tree Hill, Greenwich Park.

121

St James's Palace, scene of the royal wedding.

organ, and a gallery made for the musicians. An anthem composed by Hendel for the occasion was wretchedly sung...', wrote the Earl of Egmont.

By now desperately short of good operatic voices, Handel sent hastily to Italy to procure new singers for his forthcoming opera season, which opened on 5 May with a revival of *Ariodante* (his new opera, *Atalanta*, was not quite ready). Carestini was replaced by a new male soprano, Gioacchino Conti, known as 'Gizziello'. The *London Daily Post* reported that his début was 'met with an uncommon Reception; and in Justice both as to Voice and Judgment, he may truly be esteem'd one of the best Performers in this Kingdom'. A week later, *Atalanta* was premièred in the presence of the royal family, with Strada and Conti taking the principal rôles. The *London Daily Post* described in detail the opulent set, probably painted by Joseph Goupy, later Painter and Surveyor of the Royal Cabinet to the Prince of Wales:

The Fore-part of the Scene represented an Avenue to the Temple of *Hymen*, adorn'd with Figures of several Heathen Deities. Next was a Triumphal Arch on the Top of which were the Arms of their Royal Highnesses, over which was placed a Princely Coronet. Under this Arch was the Figure of *Fame*, on a Cloud, sounding the Praise of this Happy Pair. The Names *Fredericus* and *Augusta* appear'd above in transparent Characters.

Thro' the Arch was seen a Pediment, supported by four Columns, on which stood two Cupids embracing, and supporting the Feathers, in a

122

Princely Coronet, the Royal Ensign of the Prince of Wales. At the farther end was a View of *Hymen's* Temple, and the Wings were adorn'd with the Loves and Graces bearing Hymnenaeal Torches, and putting Fire to Incense in Urns, to be offer'd up upon this joyful Union.

The opera concluded with a grand chorus, during which 'several beautiful Illuminations were display'd, which gave an uncommon Delight and Satisfaction'. (These 'illuminations' comprised a spectacular firework display, including a 'fountain of fire', and a giant Catherine wheel which threw out a shower of golden, silver and blue fiery rain.)

Despite such visual splendours, the public remained unimpressed. 'The two opera houses are, neither of them, in a successful way; and it is the confirmed opinion that this winter will complete your friend *Handel*'s destruction, as far as the loss of his money can destroy him...', wrote Benjamin Victor to the violinist Matthew Dubourg in Dublin.

On Tuesday last, we had a new opera of Handel's [probably *Atalanta*]; and at the appearance of that great prince of harmony in the orchestre, there was so universal a clap from the audience that many were surprized, and some offended at it. As to the opera, the critics say, it is too like his former compositions, and wants variety – I heard his singer [Conti] that night, and think him near equal in merit to the late *Carestini*, with this advantage, that he has acquired the happy knack of throwing out a sound, now and then, very like to what we hear from a distressed young calf... As to the Operas, they must tumble, for the King's presence could hardly hold them up, and even that prop is denied them, for his majesty will not admit his royal ears to be tickled this season. As to music, it flourishes in this place more than ever, in subscription concerts and private parties, which must prejudice all operas and public entertainments.

In this inauspicious climate, Handel opened his autumn season with revivals of *Alcina*, attended by the Prince and Princess of Wales, *Atalanta*, and *Poro*, in which the male alto Domenico Annibale made his début. Mrs Pendarves thought he combined 'the best part of Senesino's voice and Carestini's, with a prodigious fine taste and good action'. She also reported that Handel had played to her the overtures of two new operas, 'which are charming'. The first of these, *Arminio*, a story of love, military honour and the struggle for national independence set against the background of the disastrous Roman campaign of 9AD when three legions were lured into a wood on the German frontier and massacred, was premièred on 12 January 1737, with Annibale in the title rôle, but had only six performances. The following month *Giustino*, based on the career of Justinian, who rose from

123

humble farmer to become Roman Emperor, fared little better: it had six performances before the theatres closed for Lent, and three more afterwards. Burney noted that the first cadence in the opening aria, 'Un vostro sguardo', was soon afterwards copied by Arne in 'Rule Britannia!'.

During the Lenten season, Handel first introduced the custom of performing oratorios at Covent Garden every Wednesday and Friday, ending with four performances in Passion Week. 'We hear, since Operas have been forbidden being performed at the Theatre in Covent Garden on the Wednesdays and Fridays in Lent, Mr Handel is preparing Dryden's Ode of *Alexander's Feast*, the Oratorios of *Esther* and *Deborah*, with several new Concertos for the Organ and other Instruments; also an Entertainment of Musick, called *Il trionfo del Tempo e della Verità*, which Performances will be brought on the Stage and varied every Week', reported the *London Daily Post*. Unwilling to be deprived of their pleasure during Lent, fashionable audiences flocked to the new entertainment. *Alexander's Feast* was performed on 17 March, 'with great Applause, and to the Satisfaction of a numerous Audience' (*Daily Journal*), while the Prince of Wales commanded a repeat performance of Handel's organ concerto, given in the interval. A week later, again by royal command, Handel revived his old Italian oratorio *Il trionfo del Tempo e della Verità*, which had four performances, against *Esther*'s two.

On 13 April, as the opera season resumed at Covent Garden with a *pasticcio* entitled *Didone abbandonata*, Handel suffered a paralytic stroke. 'The ingenious Mr Handell is very much indispos'd, and it's thought with a Paraletick Disorder, he having at present no Use of his Right Hand, which, if he don't regain, the Publick will be depriv'd of his fine Compositions', reported the *London Evening Post* a month later. By mid-May, Handel was still too ill to be able to direct the four performances of his new opera *Berenice* – a comedy of love and politics set in ancient Egypt. Both Strada, as Queen Berenice, whose marriage plans threaten to upset the delicate balance of power held by Rome, and Conti, as her Roman suitor Alexander, made their final London appearances in *Berenice*; and on this anticlimactic note, Handel's season ended on 15 June. Four days earlier, the indisposition of Farinelli had brought the Opera of the Nobility to an equally premature end: both he and the 'Porpoise' (Porpora) left for Italy shortly afterwards.

Interlude:

The Man

Handel's general look was somewhat heavy and sour, but when he did smile, it was his sire the sun, bursting out of a black cloud. There was a sudden flash of intelligence, wit, and good humour, beaming in his countenance, which I hardly ever saw in any other. (Burney)

To his many admirers, both at home and abroad, he was Orpheus; to his colleagues he was simply 'The Man', or 'The Bear'. Myths and anecdotes abound from Handel's long public career; but virtually nothing is known of his personal life. Apart from his alleged early liaison with Vittoria Tarquini in Italy, his name was never again publicly linked with any woman's. Mattheson, in his brief biographical note on Handel in the *Grundläge einer Ehren-Pforte* (1740), noted 'One has not yet heard that he is married: albeit it were high time…'; while George III is said to have remarked that Handel's amours 'were rather of short duration, always within the pale of his own profession'. Certainly the breadth of experience contained in the operas and oratorios, especially the sympathetic treatment accorded to both male and female characters embroiled in the deadly tangles of love and jealousy, suggest a first-hand knowledge of the joys and pitfalls of human relationships.

The true reason for Handel's lack of any permanent relationship may simply have been his total devotion to work. Burney thought that 'so occupied and absorbed was HANDEL, by the study and exercise of his profession, that he had little time to bestow, either on private amusements, or the cultivation of friendship'. 'His intimate friends were but few', wrote Hawkins; 'no impertinent visits, no idle engagements to card parties, or other expedients, to kill time, were suffered to interrupt the course of his studies.' Yet Handel was not naturally reticent. He evidently enjoyed good company: during his Burlington House days, he would often play on the fine new Father Smith organ in St Paul's Cathedral after evening service, before adjourning 'to

the Queen's Arms tavern in St Paul's churchyard, where there was a great room, with a harpsichord in it; and oftentimes an evening was there spent in music and musical conversation' (Hawkins). Mrs Pendarves (née Granville), Handel's neighbour in Brook Street, described an intimate evening at her house in April 1734, when Handel was invited to join a select company of about a dozen people. 'I never was so well entertained at an opera!... Mr Handel was in the best humour in the world, and played lessons and accompanied Strada and all the ladies that sang from seven o'the clock till eleven. I gave them tea and coffee, and about half an hour after nine had a salver brought in of chocolate, mulled white wine and biscuits. Everybody was easy and seemed pleased.'

'He was in his person a large made and very portly man', wrote Hawkins. 'His gait, which was ever sauntering, was rather ungraceful, as it had in it something of that rocking motion, which distinguishes those whose legs are bowed.' Burney concurred: 'The figure of Handel was large, and he was somewhat corpulent, and unwieldy in his motions'. When he played his favourite Ruckers harpsichord, the 'keys whereof, by incessant practice, were hollowed like the bowl of a spoon' (Hawkins), Handel's 'hand was then so fat', according to Burney, 'that the knuckles, which usually appear convex, were like those of a child,

Handel's harpsichord, now in Fenton House, London.

127

dinted or dimpled in, so as to be rendered concave.' When Susanna Cibber inquired of a friend 'whether he did not think Mr HANDEL had a charming hand? [he] replied "a hand, madam! you mistake, it's a foot", – "Poh! poh! says she, has he not a fine finger?" "Toes, by G– –, madam!" '

'Nature, indeed, required a great supply of sustenance to support so huge a mass', continues Burney, 'and he was rather epicurean in the choice of it; but this seems to have been the only appetite he allowed himself to gratify.' Burney goes on to relate an incident during a dinner party held at Handel's house in Brook Street.

During the repast, HANDEL often cried out "Oh – I "have de taught"; when the company, unwilling that, out of civility to them, the public should be robbed of any thing so valuable as his musical ideas, begged he would retire and write them down; with which request, however, he so frequently complied, that, at last, one of the most suspicious had the ill-bred curiosity to peep through the keyhole into the adjoining room; where he perceived that 'dese taughts', were only bestowed on a fresh hamper of Burgundy, which as was afterwards discovered, he had received in a present from his friend, the late Lord Radnor, while his company was regaled with more generous and spirited port.

In 1754, the artist Joseph Goupy published a vicious cartoon of Handel as a pig: one of the two engraved versions bore the text:

The Charming Brute

The Figure's odd – yet who wou'd think?
Within this Tunn'of Meat and Drink
There dwells the Soul of soft Desires
And all that HARMONY inspires.

Can contrast such as this be found?
Upon the Globe's extensive Round?
There can – yon Hogshead is his Seat,
His sole Devotion is – to Eat.

The other was shorter, but equally unkind:

Strange Monsters have Adorn'd the Stage,
Not Afric's Coast produces more,
And yet no Land nor Clime nor Age,
Have equal'd this Harmonious Boar.

Handel wearing the enormous white wig for which he was renowned.

Deeply hurt by this unprovoked attack from one whom he had regarded as a personal friend, Handel is said to have cut Goupy out of his will.

Hawkins and Burney were in agreement concerning Handel's genial demeanour. Hawkins writes: 'His features were finely marked, and the general cast of his countenance placid, bespeaking dignity attempered with benevolence, and every quality of the heart that has a tendency to beget confidence and insure esteem'; while according to Burney, 'his countenance, which I remember as perfectly as that of any man I saw but yesterday, was full of fire and dignity; and such as impressed ideas of superiority and genius.'

One of Handel's most egregious features was his enormous white wig, the sort of wig which, in the words of Edward Fitzgerald, 'some great General of the day used to take off his head after the fatigue of the battle, and hand over to his valet to have the bullets combed out of it.' Even after the *beau monde* had long abandoned such encumbrances for the lighter 'Mozartian' style, with a beribboned pigtail, Handel refused to abandon his vast headpiece, whose disposition was carefully noted as a barometer of its wearer's fluctuating moods. Burney reported that when things went well at the oratorio, Handel's wig 'had a certain nod, or vibration, which manifested his pleasure and satisfaction. Without it, nice observers were certain that he was out of humour.'

Handel was no plaster saint. He swore profusely, and his fearful temper made him many enemies – not least among the unfortunate singers who frequently found themselves on the receiving end of his wrath. In rehearsal, he could be terrifying. Burney recounts:

At the close of an air, the voice with which he used to cry out, CHORUS! was extremely formidable indeed; and, at the rehearsals of his Oratorios, at Carleton-House, if the prince and princess of Wales were not exact in coming into the Music-Room, he used to be very violent; yet, such was the reverence with which his Royal Highness treated him, that, admitting HANDEL to have had cause of complaint, he has been heard to say, "Indeed, it is cruel to have kept these poor people, meaning the performers, so long from their scholars, and other concerns." But if the maids of honour, or any other female attendants, talked, during the performance, I fear that our modern Timotheus, not only swore, but called names; yet, at such times, the princess of Wales, with her accustomed mildness and benignity, used to say, "Hush! hush! HANDEL's in a passion."

'He was a blunt and peremptory disciplinarian on these occasions', wrote Burney, 'but had a humour and wit in delivering his instructions, and even in chiding and finding fault, that was peculiar to himself and extremely diverting to all but those on whom his lash was laid... He was impetuous, rough, and

130

peremptory in his manners and conversation, but totally devoid of ill-nature or malevolence; indeed, there was an original humour and pleasantry in his most lively sallies of anger or impatience, which, with his broken English, were extremely risible. His natural propensity to wit and humour, and happy method of relating common occurrences, in an uncommon way, enabled him to throw persons and things into very ridiculous attitudes...' In an age of wits, Handel's ripostes were considered so amusing as to be widely reported. In Burney's opinion, 'had he been as great a master of the English language as Swift, his *bons mots* would have been as frequent, and somewhat of the same kind'. No man ever told a story with greater humour, reported another witness, but it 'was requisite for the hearer to have a competent knowledge of at least four languages: English, French, Italian, and German; for in his narratives he made use of them all.' 'De toctor Creen is gone to the tefel!', Handel is said to have remarked drily when his arch-rival Dr Maurice Greene joined the Apollo Society, which held its meetings at the Devil Tavern in Temple Bar. Some of his wittiest sallies were at his own expense: when *Theodora* flopped, Handel wrote to its librettist, Morell, of

Dr Maurice Greene, English composer and organist (1696-1755).

the last performance, 'Will you be there next Friday night, and I will play it to you?' Burney recounts: 'Sometimes, however, I have heard him, as pleasantly as philosophically, console his friends, when, previous to the curtain being drawn up, they have lamented that the house was so empty, by saying "Nevre moind; de moosic wil sound de petter." '

He was openly contemptuous of sycophants and flatterers: he once referred to his former patron Cardinal Pamphili as 'an old Fool'. When Charles Jennens, one of his librettists, inquired 'Why Fool? because he wrote an Oratorio? perhaps you would call me fool for the same reason!', Handel retorted, 'So I would, if you flatter'd me as he did!' His sound business sense – which enabled him to make regular investments in stock as well as cash deposits in the Bank of England, and ultimately to die a very rich man by eighteenth-century standards – made him the object of envy, and he was more than once unjustly accused of fleecing the public. In fact, his financial dealings seem to have been remark-

Handel; portrait by Hudson.

Handel's organ at St
Laurence's Church,
Whitchurch, Edgware, near
Cannons.

able for their probity: he always paid his singers and players as soon as his own finances allowed. The more dubious morality of his artistic 'borrowings' – the unattributed incorporation into his own works of large sections or even complete pieces of music by other composers – has since worried biographers: as early as 1722, Handel was openly accused by his former friend Mattheson of plagiarising an aria from Mattheson's opera *Porsenna* (which Handel had directed in Hamburg), in his own *Agrippina* and *Muzio Scevola*. Although the practice was common in the eighteenth century, Handel's use of other composers' material was more open and extensive than usual, and seems to have increased in proportion to the decline of his health and productivity. However, as Winton Dean has pointed out, Handel always immeasurably enriched his 'acquisitions', thereby 'repaying his debt with compound interest'.

His private generosity towards charitable concerns also seems to have become more pronounced after his first stroke in 1737, although his first concern was naturally for the welfare of his immediate relations. When his favourite niece and goddaughter, Johanna Friderika Michaelsen, married in 1736, Handel – then in the throes of personal financial distress – sent wedding presents of a gold watch and two signet rings for the bridegroom, and a solitaire diamond ring, a 'stone of the first water and quite perfect', for the bride.

Towards the end of his life, as his illnesses and infirmities multiplied, Handel seems to have found consolation in religion. After his strict Lutheran upbringing and the heavy-handed attempts to convert him to Catholicism in Rome, he appreciated the tolerant attitude of a country 'where no man suffers any molestation or inconvenience on account of his religious principles'. 'But though he was so rough in his language, and in the habit of swearing, a vice then much more in fashion than at present, he was truly pious, during the last years of his life, and constantly attended public prayers, twice a day, winter and summer, both in London and Tunbridge' (Burney). During the last two or three years of Handel's life, Hawkins often saw him in his own parish church of St George, Hanover Square, 'on his knees, expressing by his looks and gesticulations the utmost fervour of devotion', and judged him:

a man of blameless morals, [who] throughout his life manifested a deep sense of religion. In conversation he would frequently declare the pleasure he felt in setting the Scriptures to music: and how much contemplating the many sublime passages in the Psalms had contributed to his edification; and now he found himself near his end, these sentiments were improved into solid and rational piety, attended with a calm and even temper of mind.

133

Chapter 9

New Directions

The observation that misfortunes rarely come single, was verified in Handel. His fortune was not more impaired, than his health and understanding. His right-arm was become useless to him, from a stroke of the palsy; and how greatly his senses were disordered at intervals, for a long time, appeared from an hundred instances, which are better forgotten than recorded. The most violent deviations from reason, are usually seen when the strongest faculties happen to be thrown out of course.

In this melancholic state, it was in vain for him to think of any fresh projects for retrieving his affairs. His first concern was how to repair his constitution. But tho' he had the best advice, and tho' the necessity of following it was urged to him in the most friendly manner, it was with the utmost difficulty that he was prevailed on to do what was proper, when it was any way disagreeable. For this reason it was thought best for him to have recourse to the vapor-baths of Aix-la-Chapelle [Aachen], over which he sat near three times as long as hath ever been the practice. Whoever knows any thing of the nature of those baths, will, from this instance, form some idea of his surprising constitution. His sweats were profuse beyond what can well be imagined. His cure, from the manner as well as from the quickness, with which it was wrought, passed with the Nuns for a miracle. When, but a few hours from the time of his quitting the bath, they heard him at the organ in the principal church as well as convent, playing in a manner so much beyond any they had ever been used to, such a conclusion in such persons was natural enough.

Tho' his business was so soon dispatched, and his cure judged to be thoroughly effected, he thought it prudent to continue at Aix about six weeks, which is the shortest period usually allotted for bad cases. (Mainwaring)

Handel had only been at Aix a few weeks before he returned to work, compiling a *pasticcio* (now lost) to celebrate the 500th anniversary of the town of Elbing on the Baltic. According to the Earl of Shaftesbury:

[Handel's] recovery was so compleat, that on his Return from thence to

England, he was able to play long Voluntaries upon the Organ. In one of the great Towns in Flanders, where he had asked Permission to Play, the Organist attended him, not knowing who he was; and seem'd Struck with Mr Handell's Playing when he began: But when he heard Mr Handell lead off a Fugue, in Astonishment he ran up to him, & embracing him, said "you can be no other but the great Handell".

Handel returned from his cure at the beginning of November 1737, 'greatly recovered in his Health'. On 20 November, his patron and friend Queen Caroline died. At her funeral, which took place in King Henry VII's Chapel at Westminster Abbey, on 17 December, Handel's anthem *The Ways of Zion do Mourn* was performed by a choir of around 80 voices, drawn from the choirs of the Chapel Royal, Westminster, St Paul's and Windsor, accompanied by a large orchestra of about 100 players. The Bishop of Chichester reckoned the piece 'to be as good as he ever made'; while the Duke of Chandos reported that 'the Anthem took up three quarter of an hour of the time, of which the composition was exceeding fine, and adapted very properly to the melancholly occasion of it; but I can't say so much of the performance.'

Meanwhile, the Opera of the Nobility had ceased operations, leaving the ever-hopeful Heidegger (at the King's Theatre) in sole command of Italian opera on the London stage. Heidegger had engaged a new castrato, Gaetano Majorelli (known as 'Caffarelli'), as a substitute for Farinelli; and had intended to replace Porpora with another Italian composer. However, by the new year, he and Handel were reconciled, and Handel was engaged as composer and conductor at a salary of £1,000. His physical and mental recovery seemed complete: on Christmas Eve 1737, he completed a new opera, *Faramondo*; took Christmas Day off, and on Boxing Day, began work on *Serse*. *Faramondo* – whose convoluted plot is based around the character of Pharamond, an Arthurian knight of the Round Table, said to have been an early king of France – opened on 3 January with a relatively new cast. Caffarelli took the title rôle; the French singer Elisabeth Duparc, known as '*La Francesina*', replaced Strada as the female lead; and two other newcomers, Maria Marchesini, known as '*La Lucchesina*', and the bass Antonio Lottini, sang Adolfo and Teobaldo respectively. Three singers from the Nobility Opera, including Montagnana and Merighi, returned to the fold, while the sole survivor from Handel's Covent Garden company was the English counter-tenor William Savage.

Heidegger's new cast opened at the Haymarket and 'met with general Applause. It being the First Time of Mr Handel's Appearance this Season, he was honour'd with extraordinary and

Henry Carey, librettist and composer.

repeated Signs of Approbation', reported the London press. But within a fortnight or so, the 15-year-old Lord Wentworth predicted that 'the poor operas I doubt go on badly, for tho' every body praises both Cafferielli [sic] and the opera yet it has never been full, and if it is not now at first it will be very empty towards the latter end of the winter.' Audiences were flocking to a rival attraction at Covent Garden, the clever burlesque satire on Italian opera, *The Dragon of Wantley*, with words by Carey and music by John Frederick Lampe. 'I like it vastly and the musick is excessive pretty, and th'it is a burlesque on the operas yet Mr Handel owns he thinks the tunes very well composed', reported Wentworth. On 25 February, Handel produced a new *pasticcio*, *Alessandro Severo*, with arias drawn from ten of his previous operas, but with fresh recitatives and five new arias. It had six performances, one more than *Serse*, Handel's sole attempt at a genuine comic opera, which opened on 15 April with an all-Italian cast. Although the famous opening cavatina in praise of a plane tree 'Ombra mai fù' (known to subsequent generations as 'Handel's Largo') later became one of his most celebrated melodies, the opera as a whole was a complete flop. Burney found it 'old-fashioned and lacking in inspiration' – an unfounded criticism, as recent modern revivals have shown.

Handel was still deeply in debt from his Covent Garden fiasco: it was rumoured that he was being pursued for salary arrears by Anna Strada's irate husband. On 28 March 1738, he attempted to recoup some of his losses by putting on a benefit concert at the King's Theatre, described (wrongly) as an 'Oratorio'. In fact, it offered a mixed programme of sacred and secular music, including a Chandos anthem (*As pants the Hart*) and a Coronation anthem, arias from *Deborah*, and organ concertos. The Earl of Egmont estimated the total audience at 1,300, including some 500 people accommodated on benches on the stage: Handel is reckoned to have made £1,000. Among the audience was Jonathan Tyers, manager of Vauxhall Gardens, one of the earliest and most popular of London's pleasure grounds. Opened in 1661 in the gardens of a riverside mansion in Lambeth, Vauxhall offered a variety of entertainment for a cross-section of society, including suppers served in alcoves decorated by artists of the calibre of Hogarth and Hayman, firework displays, promenades, and concerts given from covered pavilions. Tyers greatly admired Handel, whose music featured regularly in the open-air concerts at Vauxhall; and shortly after the benefit concert (for which he took 50 tickets), he commissioned a statue of the composer, to be carved from white marble by the young French sculptor Louis François Roubiliac, and placed in a 'grand Nich, erected on Purpose in the great Grove at Vaux-hall Gardens...where his

Vauxhall Gardens, the venue for many open-air concerts featuring Handel's music.

Harmony has so often charm'd even the greatest Crouds into the profoundest Calm and most decent Behaviour'. In contrast to the solemn, bewigged figure depicted by Jacob Houbraken on the frontispiece of Walsh's publication of *Alexander's Feast* (1738), Roubiliac depicted the composer in relaxed mood and casual attire (nightcap and slippers). The statue was inaugurated on May 1, when the gardens opened for the summer season. The *London Daily Post* reported:

> The several Pieces of Music play'd on that Occasion had never [been] heard before in the Garden... The Company express'd great Satisfaction at the Marble Statue of Mr *Handel*, who is represented in a loose Robe, stroking the Lyre, and listening to the Sounds; which a little Boy, carv'd at his Feet, seems to be writing down on the back of the Violoncello [in fact, he is writing on manuscript paper balanced on the back of the instrument]. The whole Composition is in a very elegant Taste.

The statue, which cost Tyers £300, represented a most unusual and touching tribute to a living composer. After the closure of Vauxhall in the mid-nineteenth century, it stood for many years in the foyer of Novello's music shop in Wardour Street before its eventual removal to the Victoria and Albert Museum.

Despite his own relatively impoverished state, Handel, too, could still be generous. The failure of the two opera companies in the summer of 1737 must have left many musicians unemployed. One of these, an oboist of Dutch origin named Jean

137

Christian Kytch, who had been closely associated with Handel –
he played in the Cannons orchestra, then in the King's Theatre
opera band, and gave many public concerts featuring Handel's
solo wind music – had recently died, leaving his widow and family
destitute. Shortly afterwards, several of Kytch's former colleagues
were horrified to see his two small sons, starving and neglected,
'driving milk asses through the Haymarket' to earn a few pennies.
To assist the bereaved family, they immediately set up a fund
which soon acquired the aim of helping all 'decayed musicians
and their families'. The first meeting of this society, which was to
develop into the Royal Society of Musicians of Great Britain,
took place at the Crown and Anchor Tavern on 23 April 1738,
and numbered among its subscribers, Boyce, Arne, Greene,
Pepusch and Handel, who thereafter organised an annual oratorio
performance for its benefit.

While Heidegger tried – and failed – to raise subscriptions for
another opera season, Handel, dejected by repeated failures,

turned his attention back to oratorio. In the summer of 1735, he had received a letter from the amateur writer Charles Jennens, who had subscribed for every score which Handel's publishers had issued since 1725. Jennens had sent Handel an oratorio text (thought to be *Saul*), which Handel promised to peruse when leisure allowed. Towards the end of July 1738, he resurrected this libretto, and began work on the new oratorio. In September, Jennens paid Handel a visit, and found him full of 'maggots' (improbable ideas) for the production of *Saul*:

Mr Handel's head is more full of maggots than ever. I found yesterday in his room a very queer instrument which he calls carillon (*Anglice*, a bell) and says some call it a Tubalcain [the Old Testament smith], I suppose because it is both in the make and tone like a set of Hammers striking upon anvils. 'Tis played upon with keys like a Harpsichord and with this Cyclopean instrument he designs to make poor Saul stark mad. His second maggot is an organ of £500 price which (because he is overstocked with money) he has bespoke of one Moss [Jonathan Morse] of Barnet. This organ, he says, is so constructed that, as he sits at it he has a better command of his performers than he used to have, and he is highly delighted to think with what exactness his Oratorio will be performed by the help of this organ; so that for the future instead of beating time at his oratorios, he is to sit at the organ all the time with his back to the Audience. His third maggot is a Hallelujah which he has trump'd up at the end of his oratorio since I went into the Country, because he thought the conclusion of the oratorio not Grand enough; tho' if that were the case 'twas his own fault, for the words would have bore as Grand Musick as he could have set 'em to: but this Hallelujah, Grand as it is, comes in very nonsensically, having no manner of relation to what goes before... I could tell you more of his maggots: but it grows late and I must defer the rest till I write next, by which time, I doubt not, more new ones will breed in his Brain.

Saul, the result of all this furious activity, was completed, after much rewriting and reorganisation, on 27 September. Four days later, Handel began work on *Israel in Egypt* (to a text also thought to be by Jennens), which was to be prefaced by his funeral anthem for Queen Caroline. In the new year, Handel hired the King's Theatre for a short run of 12 nights; and on 16 January 1739, *Saul* received its first performance to the accompaniment of a huge orchestra including carillon, organ and a pair of the 'largest kettle-drums in the Tower [of London], so to be sure it will be most excessive noisy with a bad set of singers', wrote Lord Wentworth. The events of the oratorio take place after David's victory over Goliath. The adulation accorded to the young hero arouses King Saul's jealous anger, and in a fit of fury ('A serpent in my bosom warm'd'), Saul hurls his javelin at David, and then commands his son Jonathan to kill his friend. After repeated attempts on David's life have misfired, Saul consults the Witch of Endor, who foretells the King's death in battle. The bodies of Saul and Jonathan, who dies at his father's side, are borne in solemn procession during the famous 'Dead March', and the oratorio concludes with a stirring call to arms, encouraging David to 'retrieve the Hebrew name'.

The royal children attended the première of *Saul*, which was 'met with general Applause by a numerous and splendid Audience'. Encouraged by the success which had been denied him for so long, Handel revived *Alexander's Feast* and *Il trionfo del Tempo e della Verità*; followed by *Israel in Egypt* on 4 April. Despite Handel's vivid depiction in the five famous 'Plague Choruses', of the various epidemics which afflict Egypt – including darkness, hailstones, insects and death of the first-born – *Israel in Egypt* was a complete failure. Its excessive length diluted the dramatic impact of the Exodus story, and strong objections were raised to the use of a biblical text. The work found defenders: one anonymous correspondent declared, 'I never yet met with any Musical Performance, in which the Words and Sentiments were so thoroughly studied, and so clearly understood; and as the Words are taken from the Bible, they are perhaps some of the most sublime parts of it. I was indeed concern'd, that so excellent a Work of so great a Genius was neglected, for tho' it was a Polite and attentive Audience, it was not large enough I doubt to encourage him in any future Attempt.' For the second performance on April 11, Handel hastily cut out several of the choruses, replacing some with Italian numbers taken from previous works, but the public remained unmoved. *Israel* had only three performances, and subsequent revivals proved equally unsuccessful: it was not until Queen Victoria's reign that the oratorio's high proportion of choruses and colourful orchestration finally established it as second only to *Messiah* in the affection of choral societies and music-lovers. Two performances of *Giove in Argo*, a little-known *pasticcio*-opera cobbled together from Handel's earlier works, brought the season to an early close.

While Handel's stage works seemed to be suffering a temporary eclipse, his instrumental music was rapidly gaining popularity. A set of six organ concertos, which Handel continued to perform to great acclaim between the acts of his operas and oratorios, had been published by Walsh in October 1738, printed 'from Mr Handel's original Manuscript and corrected by Himself' – apparently in response to a 'mangled edition' issued by an unknown pirate. In January 1739, Walsh had issued a set of seven trio sonatas, Op.5, for two violins or flutes and *continuo*; and on 21 April 1740, a set of 12 new 'Grand Concerto's' made their appearance in print, under the protection of a new royal copyright privilege. Handel's original 14-year privilege had expired five years earlier, shortly before the death of John Walsh senior; and while complete dramatic works were less attractive to pirates, instrumental pieces, aimed at the music-loving middle classes, were easy prey. Handel therefore sought further protection, and the Concertos – his last works to be issued on subscription – were accordingly published 'With his Majesty's Royal Licence and Protection' by Walsh's heir and successor, John Walsh Jr. The list of 100 subscribers was headed by George II's six offspring; while several individuals, among them Jonathan Tyers and Charles Jennens, ordered multiple copies of these *concerti grossi*, cast in the old-fashioned Italian mould of Corelli, yet as full of fresh and innovative ideas as Bach's *Brandenburg Concertos*, with which they may easily stand comparison.

In the meantime, one Robert Jenkins, captain of an English merchant ship, had had his ear torn off by Spanish marauders in 1738. The outrage caused by his production of the severed organ in the House of Commons forced Walpole to declare war on Spain – the so-called 'War of Jenkins' Ear', which later escalated to become part of the wider War of the Austrian Succession – on 19 October 1739. To add to the national misery, a spell of intense cold weather had set in by mid-November, presaging the most severe winter Britain had experienced for many years. The Thames froze over, and bonfires were lit on the ice. On St Cecilia's Day, *Alexander's Feast*, together with *From harmony, from heav'nly harmony*, a new Cecilian ode to words by Dryden, were performed at the Theatre Royal in Lincoln's Inn Fields, hired by Handel for the season. 'Particular Preparations are making to keep the House warm; and the Passage from the Fields to the House will be cover'd for better Conveniency', reported the *London Daily Post*. The combination of harsh weather and the war robbed Londoners of other entertainment: in December, Richard West complained to Horace Walpole, 'Plays we have none, or damned ones. Handel has had a concerto [concert season] this winter. No opera, no nothing. All for war and Admiral Haddock [commander of the British fleet in the Mediterranean].' On 6 February, a scheduled revival of *Acis* had to be postponed 'in consideration of the Weather continuing so cold', but in spite of 'Particular Care…taken to have the House survey'd and secur'd against the Cold, by having Curtains plac'd before every Door, and constant Fires…kept in the House 'till the Time of Performance', a further deferral proved necessary owing to the illness of two principal singers. The same precautions were taken at the end of the month for the première of a new work, the ode *L'Allegro, il Penseroso ed il Moderato* (to a text adapted by Jennens). The first two parts, based on Milton, take the form of a dispute between hedonists intent on the giddy pursuit of pleasure and those who prefer a calmer, more rational approach to life. To these, Jennens, perhaps unwisely, added his own resolution, advocating a policy of moderation. This third part, which was often dropped in subsequent performances, may have been Handel's idea: in 1742, Jennens wrote to a friend:

A little piece I wrote at Mr Handel's request to be subjoyn'd to Milton's *Allegro and Penseroso*, to which he gave the name of *Il Moderato*, and which united those two independent Poems in one Moral Design, met with smart censures from I don't know who. I overheard one in the Theatre saying it was Moderato indeed, and the Wits at Tom's Coffee House honour'd it with the name of "Moderatissimo".

John Milton (1608-74).

L'Allegro was generally much admired: an extravagant panegyric appeared in the *Gentleman's Magazine* of May 1740:

If e'er *Arion's* music calm'd the floods.
And *Orpheus* ever drew the dancing woods;
Why do not *British* trees and forest throng
To hear the sweeter notes of *Handel's* song?

Thou, sovereign of the lyre, dost so excel,
Who against thee, against thy art rebel.
But uncontested is in song, thy sway;
Thee all the nations where 'tis known obey:
E'en *Italy*, who long usurp'd the lyre,
Is proud to learn thy precepts and admire.
What harmony she had thou thence didst bring
And imp'd thy genius with a stronger wing;
To form thee, talent, travel, art, combine,
And all the powers of music now are thine.

During the summer of 1740, Handel visited the Continent; and, on returning, he made two last attempts at Italian opera. On 10 October, he finished *Imeneo*, which opened at Lincoln's Inn Fields on 22 November, followed by *Deidamia* on 10 January 1741. Despite two new Italian singers (the male soprano Andreoni, and Signora Monza, whom Mrs Pendarves described as having a voice between 'Cuzzoni's and Strada's – strong but not harsh, her person *miserably bad*, being very low and *excessively* crooked'), both operas were total failures.

On 10 February 1741, with the last performance of *Deidamia*, Handel's 30-year reign on the London operatic stage – during which he had presented 40 operas – came to a melancholy end. 'During my first visit to London, in the year 1736, I found two Italian opera companies there', wrote a German diplomat.

The celebrated Mr Hendel directed the one, and had as his principal singers Signor Conti-Giziello and Signora Strada, as well as a fine bass. Apart from that his opera-house was noted for the quality of the music, which was beautifully written. This English Orpheus directed the proceedings himself. But he had a formidable rival, Mr Heidegger, the manager of another opera company at the *Heymarket* Theatre. The latter offered the public the best works of Messrs Hasse and Porpora and had them performed by Messrs Farinelli, Senesino and Madame Cuzzoni. The eminent skill of the composers, the extraordinary quality of the voices, the rivalry between performers – all this made London then the centre of the musical world. But today it seems that Eurterpe has abandoned Albion's shores leaving nothing but the Oratorio, that is, a kind of sacred concert, which Mr Hendel sometimes puts on.

Despite many reverses, Handel had clung doggedly to his first love, Italian opera. The reason for his ultimate failure lay in the coarsening of public taste, and a gradual change in the composition of theatre audiences. Baroque opera, dealing largely with the exploits of gods and heroes of mythology and ancient history, was primarily designed as an aristocratic entertainment, intended to inspire its courtly audience to heroic feats of emulation. Noted for their xenophobia, English audiences, who included an increasing number of middle-class patrons, tolerated this 'exotic and irrational entertainment' (in Dr Johnson's famous words) largely for the novelty of its performing 'animals', particularly the castrati – the 'fat capons', who were regarded primarily as interesting freaks. So far as the drama itself was concerned, the English of all social classes preferred to hear their native tongue, particularly in popular comedy or melodrama dealing with real-life situations and believable characters. This demand for more naturalistic, vernacular entertainment was by no means confined to England: by the mid-century the comic *intermezzi* between the acts of Italian operas had drained the life from their serious hosts; while in France, the numerous operatic parodies improvised by strolling players at the Parisian Fair theatres led to the parallel decline of the courtly edifice of *tragédie-lyrique*. Even though Handel's operas continued to be prized by discerning connoisseurs, who appreciated their musical superiority, they were too subtle for average taste. If such a musically literate and knowledgeable critic as Dr Burney could regard operas primarily as a string of varied arias, designed to show off the particular vocal techniques of the principal singers, what hope was there for Handel's carefully constructed scenes, sensitively underpinning the drama with a finely-honed balance of recitative, aria and instrumental sinfonias, and – despite acrimonious disagreements – never subverted by the demands of his soloists?

None-the-less, the indifference of British audiences to Handel provoked outrage among genuine music-lovers. An anonymous defence appeared in the *London Daily Post* on 4 April 1741:

…[Handel] has charmed me from my Childhood to this Day, and as I have been so long his Debtor for one of the greatest Joys our Nature is capable of, I thought it a Duty incumbent upon me at this Time, when it is become a Fashion to neglect him, (unknown as his Person is to me) to recommend him to the public Love and Gratitude of this great City, who have, with me, so long enjoyed the Harmony of his Composition. *Cotsoni, Faustina, Cenosini,* and *Farinelli,* have charmed our Ears: We ran mad after them, and entered into Parties for the one or other with as much Vehemence as if the State had been at Stake. Their Voice indeed was grateful to the Ear; but it was *Handel* gave the Persuasion; it was his Composition that touched the Soul, and hurried us into the mad Extremes of Party-Rage for the particular Performers. His Influence prevailed, tho' his Power was invisible; and the Singer had the Praise and Profit, while the Merit, unobserved and almost unrewarded, was the poor, but the proud Lot of the forgotten Master...

And shall we then, after so many Years Possession, upon a single Disgust, upon a *faux pas* made, but not meant, so interely abandon him, as to let him Want in a Country he has so long served? in a Country of publick Spirit, where the polite Arts are in so high Esteem, and where Gratitude and Rewards have so remarkably accompanied the Merit of those who have excelled in them, that the great Genius's of other Countries have often even regretted that Part of their Fate, which gave them Birth in any other Place. It cannot be! if we are not careful for him, let us be for our own long-possessed Credit and Character in the polite World; and if old Age and Infirmity; if even a Pride so inseparable from great Men...if even such a Pride has offended, let us take it as the natural Foible of the great Genius, and let us overlook them like Spots upon the Sun, which, Spots as they are, do not eclipse or obscure his great Talent.

...I wish I could urge this Apology to its full Efficacy, and persuade the Gentlemen who have taken Offence at any Part of this great Man's Conduct (for a great Man he must be in the Musical World, whatever his Misfortunes may now too late say to the contrary:) I wish I could persuade them, I say, to take him back into Favour, and relieve him from the cruel Persecution of those little Vermin, who, taking Advantage of their Displeasure, pull down even his Bills as fast as he has them pasted up; and use a thousand other little Arts to injure and distress him. I am sure when they weigh the Thing without Prejudice, they will take him back into Favour; but in the mean time, let the Publick take Care that he wants not: That would be an unpardonable Ingratitude; and as this Oratorio of *Wednesday* next [*L'Allegro*] is his last for this Season, and if Report be true, probably his last for ever in this Country, let them, with a generous and friendly Benevolence, fill this his last House, and shew him on his Departure, that *London*, the greatest and richest City in the World, is great and rich in Virtue, as well as Money, and can pardon and forget the Failings, or even the Faults of a great Genius.

This eloquent appeal to national pride may have worked, since the performance of *L'Allegro, ed il Penseroso* (*Il Moderato* being omitted in favour of Dryden's Cecilian ode *From harmony*) was attended by 'all the fashionable people'. It was certainly seen as a farewell: Handel apparently intended to leave England, perhaps for good.

Chapter 10

Messiah

Dublin, though a place much worse than London, is not so bad as Iceland. (Dr Johnson)

Despite his bitter disappointments, Handel did not leave England after all. Over the summer of 1741, he remained in London, composing Italian duets, while his songs and instrumental pieces continued to be played at the London pleasure gardens, especially at Cuper's Gardens on the south bank of the Thames, opposite Somerset House – where music by Corelli, Hasse and others featured at regular Saturday-evening concerts. On 18 July, Handel's 'celebrated Fire Musick', originally written for the opera *Atalanta*, was performed there 'with great Applause; the Fire-works consisting of Fire-wheels, Fountains, large Sky Rockets, with an Addition of the Fire-Pump, &c.'

Handel seemed in good health and spirits, and distanced himself from operatic activity. 'He laughs very much at the opera which is preparing for next winter. He has refused to have anything to do in the matter', reported Thomas Dampier. Lord Middlesex and seven other noble subscribers were intending to restart another opera season at the King's Theatre in the Haymarket, with Galuppi as composer-in-residence and an all-Italian cast. On 31 October, Handel attended the first night of the new season, a *pasticcio*-opera *Alessandro in Persia*, with music by at least six different Italian composers. However, he did not stay long enough to witness its unexpected success (it achieved 21 performances over two seasons), since, by early November, he was on his way to Dublin, at the invitation of the Duke of Devonshire, William Cavendish, Lord Lieutenant of Ireland.

At that time under British rule, Dublin in the mid-eighteenth century had expanded into a gracious city of elegant Georgian town-houses framing well-cultivated garden squares, inhabited by an affluent, leisured Anglo-Irish ruling class. Under such favourable conditions, the arts flourished. Shortly after the

146

View of Dublin from
Phoenix Park.

Restoration, Dublin acquired its first permanent theatre in
Smock Alley, which remained the only principal playhouse until
challenged between 1734 and 1750 by the larger stage of the
Aungier Street theatre. From 1731 onwards, concerts were held
at the Crow Street Musick Hall, opened at the request of the
'Musical Academy for the practice of Italian Music', and at Mr
Neale's Great Musick Hall in Fishamble Street, built and owned
by the music publishers John and William Neale, which opened
shortly before Handel's arrival, on 2 October 1741. Although
Italian opera did not reach Dublin until the 1760s, operas in
English (including *The Beggar's Opera*) met with great success
from the 1720s onwards. Dublin's thriving concert life proved a
magnet for many foreign musicians, several of whom made their
homes there: they included the celebrated Italian violinist
Geminiani and his pupil Matthew Dubourg (Handel's close
friend), who, in 1728, succeeded J.S. Kusser (formerly impresario at the Hamburg opera) as Master and Composer of State
Music in Ireland. From 1735 onwards, Dubourg also worked for
the Prince of Wales, and often visited England. During Handel's
visit to Dublin, Dubourg led the orchestra and performed solos
during the intervals. Burney reports that one night:

Dubourg having a solo part in a song, and a close [cadenza] to make,
ad libitum, he wandered about in different keys a great while, and
seemed indeed a little bewildered, and uncertain of his original...but at

147

The Music Hall in
Fishamble Street, Dublin.

length, coming to the shake, which was to terminate this long close,
HANDEL, to the great delight of the audience, and augmentation of
applause, cried out loud enough to be heard in the most remote parts
of the theatre: "You are welcome home, Mr Dubourg!"

Dublin had a distinguished reputation for philanthropy: fund-
raising concerts were regularly given by charities for the institu-
tionalised support of the needy, sick, or imprisoned poor. Chief
among such foundations was Mercer's Hospital, opened in 1734.
Handel's sacred music was first heard in Dublin on 20 March
1736, at a concert given 'for the Benefit of Mercer's Charitable
Hospital in Stephen-Street, towards the Maintenance and Support of the distressed sick Poor'. His *Utrecht Te Deum* and *Jubilate*,
and an unidentified coronation anthem were performed by the
'best publick Performers in this Kingdom' (the choristers and
vicars-choral from the two Anglican cathedrals, Christ Church,
and St Patrick's), assisted by 'about forty Gentlemen, skilled in
Musick on various Instruments'. Similar performances were
given annually over the next five years, featuring such Handelian

148

works as the coronation, wedding and Chandos anthems, *Acis and Galatea*, the two Cecilian odes, *Deborah* and *Esther*, and *L'Allegro ed il Penseroso*.

On 21 November, the *Dublin Gazette* announced that 'last Wednesday [the 18th] the celebrated Dr Handell arrived here in the Packet-boat from Holyhead, a Gentleman universally known by his excellent Compositions in all Kinds of Musick, and particularly for his *Te Deum*, *Jubilate*, *Anthems*, and other Compositions in Church Musick (of which for some Years past have principally consisted the Entertainments in the Round Church [St Andrew's] which have so greatly contributed to support the Charity of Mercer's-Hospital) to perform his Oratorio's, for which purpose he hath engaged...several... of the best Performers in the Musical Way.'

Among these performers were two singers from London, Christina Avoglio and Thomas Arne's sister, Susanna Cibber; together with an organist called Maclaine and his soprano wife, whom Handel had recruited during an enforced stay in Chester while waiting for the wind to change for his journey across the Irish Sea.

On 10 December, Handel's *Utrecht Te Deum* and *Jubilate* and one of the Coronation Anthems were performed at St Andrew's Church for the benefit of Mercer's Hospital: Handel also gave an organ recital. Four days later, the *Dublin Journal* announced that subscription tickets for 'six Musical Entertainments for the New Musick-Hall in Fishamble street' were on sale at Handel's lodgings in Abbey Street (the house still stands today). The first of these 'entertainments', consisting of *L'Allegro, il Penseroso ed il Moderato*, two *concerti grossi* and an organ concerto, took place on 23 December, and according to the *Dublin Journal*, was 'crowded with a more numerous and polite Audience than was ever seen upon the like Occasion. The Performance was superior to any Thing of the Kind in this Kingdom before; and our Nobility and Gentry to show their Taste for all Kinds of Genius, expressed their great Satisfaction, and have already given all imaginable Encouragement to this grand Musick.' Gratified by his reception, Handel wrote to Jennens at the end of December that his concerts were sold out in advance ('I needed not to sell one single Ticket at the Door'), and that he had been pleased both with the singers and instrumentalists:

as for the Instruments they are really excellent, Mr Dubourgh beeng at the Head of them, and the Musick sounds delightfully in this charming Room, which puts me in such Spirits (and my Health being so good) that I exert my self on my Organ with more than usual Success. I opened with the Allegro, Penseroso & Moderato and I assure you that the words of the Moderato are vastly admired. The Audience being composed (besides the Flower of Ladyes of Distinction and other People of the greatest Quality) of so many Bishops, Deans, Heads of the Colledge, the most eminent People in the Law as the Chancellor, Auditor General, &tc. all which are very much taken with the Poetry... I cannot sufficiently express the kind treatment I receive here, but the Politeness of this generous Nation cannot be unknown to You, so I let You judge of the satisfaction I enjoy, passing my time with Honnour, profit and pleasure.

Further performances of *L'Allegro, Acis and Galatea, Esther* and the Cecilian ode *From harmony* took place in January and early February, when a second series of six concerts was announced, beginning with *Alexander's Feast* and *Imeneo*. On 27 March 1742, the *Dublin Journal* made the following announcement:

For Relief of the Prisoners in the several Gaols, and for the Support of Mercer's Hospital in Stephen's Street and of the Charitable Infirmary on the Inns Quay, on Monday the 12th of April, will be performed at the Musick Hall in Fishamble Street, Mr *Handel's new Grand Oratorio, call'd the* MESSIAH, in which the Gentlemen of the Choirs of both Cathedrals will assist, with some Concertoes on the Organ, by Mr Handell.

This was the first public mention of Handel's new work, composed the previous summer. In July 1741, Charles Jennens had written to his friend Edward Holdsworth: 'Handel says he will do nothing next Winter, but I hope I shall persuade him to set another Scripture Collection I have made for him, & perform it for his own Benefit in Passion week. I hope he will lay out his whole Genius & Skill upon it, that the Composition may excell all his former Compositions, as the subject excells every other Subject. The Subject is Messiah.' Spurred on by the unexpected incentive of performances in Dublin, Handel had completed the work in just 24 days.

The première of the world's most famous oratorio took place on 13 April 1742: the theatre was so packed that the ladies were requested to come 'without Hoops' – the rigid wire or bone structures which supported the elaborate dresses of the period – and the gentlemen 'without Swords', which enabled an extra 100 people to find seats. Signora Avoglio and Susanna Cibber took the soprano and mezzo solo parts, with male voices drawn from the two cathedral choirs. *Messiah* met with an ecstatic reception. 'Words are wanting to express the exquisite Delight it afforded to the admiring crouded Audience', raved the *Dublin Journal*. 'The Sublime, the Grand, and the Tender, adapted to the most elevated, majestick and moving Words, conspired to transport

Manuscript page of the *Hallelujah Chorus* from *Messiah*.

Manuscript page of the *Hallelujah Chorus* from *Messiah*.

and charm the ravished Heart and Ear…There were about 700 People in the Room, and the Sum collected…amounted to about £400, of which £127 goes to each of the three great and Pious Charities.'

In Winton Dean's words: '*Messiah* owes its unique reputation, not so much to its musical excellence – Handel wrote half a dozen oratorios as fine or finer – as to the chance that it sums up to perfection and with the greatest eloquence the religious faith, ethical, congregational, and utterly unmystical, of the average Englishman' (*Grove 6*). Jennens and Handel intended the work as 'a fine entertainment' with an edifying message wrapped up in appealing musical language. Part One is a meditation on the Incarnation, beginning with the Old Testament prophecies of the birth of Christ and ending with a reflection on the benefits of Divine love – 'He shall feed his flock like a shepherd'. Part Two deals with Christ's Passion, death and resurrection, again treated in contemplative, rather than narrative style, with the emphasis placed on mankind's burden of guilt: 'He was despised and rejected of men'. Sorrow gives way to rejoicing and Part Two concludes with the mighty *Hallelujah Chorus*. Part Three is concerned with the Second Coming. In one of Handel's most famous arias, the soprano announces, 'I know that my Redeemer liveth and shall stand at the latter day upon the earth', while the chorus contrasts 'death in Adam' with the promise of resurrection made implicit by a 'life in Christ'. The famous bass aria 'The trumpet shall sound', with its demanding *obbligato*, heralds the

151

Last Judgment; and the triumph of eternal life is jubilantly celebrated in the final chorus to a text from Revelation, 'Worthy is the Lamb that was slain, and has redeemed us to God'.

Handel consolidated his success with a performance of *Saul* on 25 May, and a further performance of *Messiah* on 3 June. At the end of the month, Thomas Arne and his wife Cecilia arrived in Dublin, where, on 21 July, Mrs Arne and her sister-in-law Susanna Cibber gave a benefit concert of Handel's music at the Fishamble Street Music Hall. At the same time, the great actor David Garrick arrived in Dublin to play Hamlet at the Smock Alley Theatre, where Handel is said to have seen him on 12 August. The next day, Handel took his leave of Jonathan Swift, Dean of St Patrick's Cathedral – an old associate of his Burlington House days. Racked by a degenerative illness, Swift's once brilliant and incisive mind now appeared to teeter on the brink of insanity. A famous anecdote quoted in Letitia Pilkington's memoirs recalls how Swift:

David Garrick in the rôle of Richard III.

fell into a deep Melancholy, and knew no body; I was told the last sensible Words he uttered, were on this Occasion: Mr Handel, when

Jonathan Swift in a portrait by Charles Servas painted in 1718.

about to quit Ireland went to take his leave of him: The Servant was a considerable Time, e'er he could make the Dean understand him; which, when he did, he cry'd, "Oh! a German, and a Genius! A Prodigy! admit him." The Servant did so, just to let Mr Handel behold the Ruins of the greatest Wit that ever lived along the Tide of Time, where all at length are lost.

On 13 August, Handel embarked for England, arriving back at the end of the month. In a letter to Jennens, he affirmed his intention (never realised) of returning to Dublin for a second oratorio season the following year; but in the meantime, he reached a new agreement with Rich to take the Covent Garden theatre for a Lenten season of oratorios, under the patronage of the Prince of Wales. The season opened on 18 February 1743 with *Samson*, an adaptation (from Milton's dramatic poem *Samson Agonistes*) of the biblical story, from Samson's blinding and degradation by the Philistines, to the apocalyptic conclusion when he regains his strength to pull down the Philistine temple on the heads of his enemies. *Samson* proved one of Handel's greatest successes, through its fusion of 'the Solemnity of Church-Musick' with 'the most pleasing Airs of the Stage' – airs such as 'Let the bright Seraphim', with its jubilant trumpet *obbligato*; Samson's recitative and aria 'Why does the God of Israel sleep?', and Dalila's hypocritically tender air 'With plaintive notes'. The words of the blind poet, particularly when lamenting his hero's loss of sight, moved the composer profoundly: an anecdote retailed by William Shields in 1800 relates that 'when Handel's servant used to bring him his chocolate in a morning, he often stood with silent astonishment (until it was cold) to see his master's tears mixing with the ink, as he penned his divine notes; which are surely as much the pictures of a sublime mind as Milton's words.' Over a decade later, when Handel too had gone blind, he never ceased, according to Burney, to become distressed and agitated during the aria 'Total eclipse', whose words, sung by the blinded and captive Samson in the public square at Gaza, epitomised his own pitiful condition.

The part of Samson – the first major dramatic rôle for tenor voice outside France – was taken by Mr Beard, with Mrs Clive (a singer from the Drury Lane playhouse) as Dalila, and Susanna Cibber as Micah. Handel played a new organ concerto in the interval, and Matthew Dubourg, temporarily back in London, played a 'Solo on the Violin' from the fourth performance onwards. *Samson* was a great success, attracting audiences away from Lord Middlesex's opera company, and even from Heidegger's annual carnival entertainments (known as 'ridottos') at the Haymarket Theatre.

Horace Walpole wrote to a friend:

Handel has set up an Oratorio against the Operas, and succeeds. He has hired all the goddesses from farces and the singers of *Roast Beef* [a popular ballad] from between the acts at both theatres, with a man with one note in his voice, and a girl without ever an one; and so they sing, and make brave hallelujahs; and the good company encore the recitative, if it happens to have any cadence like what they call a tune.

News of *Samson*'s success (it had eight performances in its first season) soon reached Dublin via an anonymous correspondent:

Our friend Mr Handell is very well, and Things have taken a quite different Turn here from what they did some Time past; for the Publick will no longer be imposed on by Italian Singers, and some wrong Headed Undertakers of bad Opera's, but find out the Merit of Mr Handell's Composition and English Performances: That Gentleman is more esteemed now than ever. The new Oratorio (called SAMSON)...has been performed four Times to more crouded Audiences than ever were seen; more People being turned away for Want of Room each Night than hath been at the Italian Opera. Mr Dubourg (lately arrived from Dublin) performed at the last, and played a Solo between the Acts, and met with universal and uncommon Applause from the Royal Family and the whole Audience.

On 19 March, Handel announced the forthcoming London première of *Messiah*, tactfully named only as 'A New Sacred Oratorio'. He had good reason for caution: on the same day, a letter appeared in the *Universal Spectator*, from a 'profess'd Lover of Musick' and a 'great Admirer of Church Musick', denouncing the practice of performing oratorios, set to sacred words, for 'diversion and amusement' in playhouses, sung by 'a Set of People very unfit to perform so solemn a Service'; and citing the forthcoming performance of *Messiah* as a prime example of this profanity. Four days later, *Messiah* made its London début – its cool reception in striking contrast to the rapture with which Dublin had greeted it. A 'reply' to the criticism voiced in the *Universal Spectator* appeared in the *Daily Advertiser* of 31 March, the last day of the oratorio season:

> N B Every, Ticket will admit either one Gentleman, or Two Ladies.
>
> ## COVENT-GARDEN.
> ### By SUBSCRIPTION.
> *The Ninth Night.*
>
> AT the Theatre-Royal in Covent-Garden, Wednesday next, will be perform'd
> ### A New Sacred ORATORIO.
> A CONCERTO on the ORGAN,
> And a Solo on the Violin by Mr. DUBOURG.
> Tickets will be deliver'd to Subscribers on Tuesday next, at Mr Handel's House in Brook-street.
> Pit and Boxes to be put together, and no Person to be admitted without Tickets, which will be deliver'd that Day, at the Office in Covent-Garden Theatre, at Half a Guinea each. First Gallery 5 s. Upper Gallery 3 s. 6 d.
> The Galleries will be open'd at Four o'Clock. Pit and Boxes at Five.
>
> *For the Benefit and Increase of a* FUND *establish'd for the Support of Decay'd* MUSICIANS, *or their Families.*

The announcement of the first London performance of *Messiah* as it appeared in the *Daily Press*.

On Mr HANDEL's new ORATORIO
perform'd at the Theatre Royal in Covent Garden

Cease, Zealots, cease to blame these Heav'nly Lays,
For Seraphs fit to sing Messiah's Praise!
Nor, for your trivial Argument, assign,
"The Theatre not fit for Praise Divine."

These hallow'd Lays to Musick give new Grace,
To Virtue Awe, and sanctify the Place;
To Harmony, like his, Celestial Pow'r is giv'n,
T'exalt the Soul from Earth, and make, of Hell, a Heav'n.

The custom – still observed – of 'All standing' during the *Hallelujah Chorus* may have dated from *Messiah*'s first London performance: a letter written in 1780 by James Beattie to the Reverend Dr Laing relates two anecdotes, 'lately heard' by Beattie:

When Handel's *Messiah* was first performed, the audience was exceedingly struck and affected by the music in general; but when that chorus struck up, "For the Lord God Omnipotent reigneth", they were so transported, that they all, together with the king (who happened to be present), started up, and remained standing till the chorus ended: and hence it became the fashion in England for the audience to stand while that part of the music is performing. Some days after the first exhibition of the same divine oratorio, Mr Handel came to pay his respect to Lord Kinnoull, with whom he was particularly acquainted. His lordship, as was natural, paid him some compliments on the noble entertainment which he had lately given the town. "My lord", said Handel, "I should be sorry if I only entertained them. I wish to make them better."

Among *Messiah*'s detractors was its librettist Charles Jennens, who, annoyed that Handel had chosen Dublin rather than London for the première, confessed himself bitterly disappointed with Handel's treatment of his text – 'being set in great haste, tho' he said he would be a year about it, & make it the best of all his Compositions. I shall put no more Sacred Words into his hands, to be thus abus'd.' Shortly before the première of *Messiah*, Jennens continued to vent his spleen:

As to the *Messiah*, 'tis still in his power by retouching the weak parts to make it fit for a publick performance; & I have said a great deal to him on the Subject; but he is so lazy & so obstinate, that I much doubt the Effect…What adds to my chagrin is, that if he makes his Oratorio ever so perfect, there is a clamour about Town, said to arise from the Brs [the Methodist Brethren, whose puritanism was gaining much ground among the middle classes] against performing it… Last Friday Handel perform'd his *Samson*, a most exquisite Entertainment, which tho' I heard with infinite Pleasure, yet it increas'd my resentment for his neglect of the *Messiah*...

Although *Messiah* had so far failed to gain much popularity in London, Handel had the satisfaction of seeing the discomfiture of his rivals at the King's Theatre. 'Gentlemen directors, with favourite abbés and favourite mistresses, have almost overturned the thing [Italian opera] in England', snorted Walpole. 'There is a new subscription formed for an Opera next year, to be carried on by the Dilettanti, a club, for which the nominal qualification is having been in Italy, and the real one, being drunk: the two chiefs are Lord Middlesex and Sir Francis Dashwood, who were seldom sober the whole time they were in Italy.' Handel was under pressure to resume opera composition, apparently at the behest of the Prince of Wales, among others; but on May 4, Walpole wrote again: 'We are likely at last to have no Opera next year: Handel has had a palsy, and can't compose; and the Duke of Dorset has set himself strenuously to oppose it, as Lord Middlesex is the impresario, and must ruin the house of Sackville by a course of these follies...'

Handel had suffered a second stroke in April, possibly brought on by disappointment and the stress of Jennens' vicious attacks. As before, he quickly recovered, and between 3 June and 4 July, completed the 'musical drama' *Semele*, based on a libretto by Congreve, after Ovid's *Metamorphoses*. Intended to be performed with little or no action or decor, 'after the manner of an oratorio', yet with a secular English text, this hybrid form inspired some of Handel's most appealing music. *Semele*, whose plot concerns the fatal ambition of Jupiter's young mortal mistress to see her lover in the full splendour of his heavenly majesty (a desire which results in her incineration) contains a wealth of gorgeous airs, including 'Endless pleasure, endless love', 'More sweet is that name', 'O sleep, why dost thou leave me?' and the enchanting 'Where'er you walk', in which Jupiter describes the Arcadian delights he has organised to keep his beloved contented.

Shortly after finishing it, Handel was asked to write two pieces to celebrate a major military victory. During the continuing War of the Austrian Succession, Britain allied herself with Austria against the French to ensure the succession to the Austrian throne of the Hapsburg archduchess Maria Theresa. Though sustaining heavy losses, the combined British and Hanoverian forces, led by George II in person, defeated the French army at Dettingen, on the river Main, on 27 June 1743. Handel's *Dettingen Te Deum*, with an anthem, *The King shall Rejoice*, were performed in the Chapel Royal at St James's Palace on 27 November, in the presence of the victorious monarch and his

The battle of Dettingen,
27 June 1743.

family. Mrs Pendarves (now remarried to Patrick Delany of Dublin) heard the Dettingen music in rehearsal. 'It is excessively fine, I was all rapture…everybody says it is the finest of his compositions; I am not well enough acquainted with it to pronounce that of it, but it is heavenly.'

Meanwhile, on 15 November, Lord Middlesex's opera company had revived Handel's *Alessandro* (renamed *Rossane*) with 'Dances and other Decorations entirely new' at the King's Theatre. It is not known whether Handel had any part in the production. 'The Opera is begun, but is not so well as last year', grumbled Walpole. Mrs Delany thought it 'infinitely better than any Italian opera; but it vexed me to hear some favourite songs mangled.' Handel's chief preoccupation, however, lay with his forthcoming Lenten oratorio season at Covent Garden, which opened on 10 February 1744 with *Semele*. 'I was yesterday to hear *Semele*; it is a delightful piece of music', wrote Mrs Delany. 'There is a four-part song that is delightfully pretty.'

In fact, *Semele* was at first such a success that Handel was able to deposit £650 in the bank on 14 February: for some considerable time he had been more accustomed to financial loss. However, within a fortnight of its first performance, Mrs Delany noted that *Semele* was to be replaced with *Samson*, since '*Semele* has a strong party against it, viz. the fine ladies, petit maîtres, and *Ignoramus*'s. All the opera people are enraged at Handel...' Popular opinion, always ready to accuse Handel of greed and exploitation, was now determined not to let him have his cake and eat it. 'I was last night to hear *Samson*', reported Mrs Delany on 25 February. 'Upon the whole it went off very well, but not better than last year. *Joseph*, I believe, will be next Friday... I hope it will be well received; the houses have not been crowded, but pretty full every night.' *Joseph and his Brethren*, one of Handel's dullest works, was performed on 2 March, and had three further performances. 'The oratorios fill very well, not withstanding the spite of the opera party: nine of the twelve are over', wrote Mrs Delany. The season concluded triumphantly with revivals of *Saul* and *Samson*: the latter drew an anonymous paean from the *London Magazine*:

> Rais'd by his subject, *Milton* nobly flew,
> And all Parnassus open'd to our view:
> By *Milton* fir'd, brave *Handel* strikes our ear,
> And every power of harmony we hear.
> When two such mighty artists blend their fire;
> Pour forth each charm that genius can inspire,
> The man whose bosom does not raptures feel,
> Must have no soul, or all his heart be steel.

Chapter 11
Music for the Royal Fireworks

By the summer of 1744, Handel had resumed good relations with Jennens. On 9 June, he wrote to him:

…As you do me the Honour to encourage my Musicall Undertakings, and even to promote them with a particular Kindness, I take the Liberty to trouble You with an account of what Engagement I have hitherto concluded. I have taken the Opera House in the Haymarketh, engaged, as Singers, Sigra Francesina, Miss Robinson, Beard, Reinhold, Mr Gates with his Boyes's and several of the best Chorus Singers from the Choirs, and I have some hopes that Mrs Cibber will sing for me… Now I should be extreamly glad to receive the first Act, or what is ready of the new Oratorio with which you intend to favour me, that I might employ all my attention and time, in order to answer in some measure the great obligation I lay under…

Handel was evidently anxious to repair the rift with Jennens, and for once, swallowed his pride. Having already completed *Hercules*, a further secular drama on the lines of *Semele*, with an English text by a new collaborator, the Reverend Thomas Broughton (intended to be performed, like *Semele*, without stage action), he immediately began work on the 'new Oratorio', *Belshazzar*. On 19 July, he acknowledged the receipt of Jennens' text for the first act, while also requesting that Jennens should 'point out these passages in the *Messiah* which You think require altering'. A month later, he professed himself 'greatly pleased' with the second act of *Belshazzar* and by 13 September, he was writing enthusiastically: 'Your most excellent Oratorio has given me great Delight in setting it to Musick and still engages me warmly. It is indeed a Noble Piece, very grand and uncommon; it has furnished me with Expressions, and has given me Opportunity to some very particular Ideas, besides so many great Choru's.' At the beginning of October, on receiving the third and final act, Handel wrote again:

I received the 3d Act, with a great deal of pleasure, as you can imagine, and you may believe that I think it a very fine and sublime Oratorio, only it is realy too long, if I should extend the Musick, it would last 4 Hours and more.

I retrench'd already a great deal of the Musick, that I might preserve the Poetry as much as I could, yet still it may be shortned. The Anthems come in very proprely...[Two choruses in *Belshazzar*, including the final one, were adapted from Chandos anthems].

Handel's new season opened at the King's Theatre on 3 November 1744 with a revival of *Deborah*, followed a month later by *Semele*. *Hercules* – the story of the Greek hero's demise at the hands of his jealous wife Dejanira, who sends him a robe impregnated with poison – was premièred on 5 January 1745, with the bass Reinhold in the title rôle. Party due to the indisposition of Susanna Cibber – always a popular box-office attraction – *Hercules* proved a total flop. Handel had underestimated the depth of his unpopularity, particularly as a result of his audacious plan to present oratorios at the King's Theatre, hitherto the preserve of opera. Jennens laid the blame for the fiasco squarely on Handel's over-ambition: he had relinquished his uniquely profitable Lenten oratorio season at Covent Garden, during which his 'entertainments' went unchallenged, to put on his 'English Operas' at the Haymarket 'on Saturdays during the run of Plays, Concerts, Assemblys, Drums, Routs, Hurricanes [the names given to certain types of private entertainments], & all the Madness of Town Diversions. His Opera, for want of the top Italian Voices, Action, Dresses, Scenes & Dances, which us'd to draw company, & prevent the Undertakers losing above 3 or 4 thousand pounds, had scarce half a house the first night, much less than half the second; & he has been quiet ever since.'

Handel acknowledged his failure: in a letter to the *Daily Advertiser* on 17 January, he publicly announced the abandonment of his series, and the return of subscription money:

Sir,

   Having for a Series of Years received the greatest Obligations from the Nobility and Gentry of this Nation, I have always retained a deep Impression of their Goodness. As I perceived, that joining good Sense and significant Words to Musick, was the best Method of recommending this to an English Audience; I have directed my Studies that way, and endeavour'd to shew, that the English Language, which is so expressive of the sublimest Sentiments is the best adapted of any to the full and solemn Kind of Musick. I have the Mortification now to find, that my Labours to please are become ineffectual, when my Expences are considerably greater. To what Cause I must impute the loss of the publick Favour I am ignorant, but the Loss itself I shall always lament.

In the mean time, I am assur'd that a Nation, whose Characteristick is Good Nature, would be affected with the Ruin of any Man, which was owing to his Endeavours to entertain them. I am likewise persuaded, that I shall have the Forgiveness of those noble Persons, who have honour'd me with their Patronage, and their Subscription this Winter, if I beg their Permission to stop short, before my Losses are too great to support, if I proceed no farther in my Undertaking; and if I intreat them to withdraw three Fourths of their Subscription, one Fourth Part only of my Proposal having been perform'd.

Many of Handel's subscribers responded to this humble and generous offer by refusing to withdraw their subscriptions. An anonymous poem compared Handel's fate to that of Orpheus, metaphorically torn to pieces by the wild women of Thrace – in this case the society ladies of London, who, led by Margaret Cecil, attempted to sabotage Handel's concerts by organising conflicting events such as card parties and balls:

> But chiefly ONE, of envious Kind,
> With Skin of Tyger *capuchin'd*,
> Was more implacable than all,
> And strait resolv'd poor *Orpheus* Fall;
> Whene'er he play'd, she'd make a *Drum*,
> Invite her Neighbours all to come;
> At other Times, wou'd send about,
> And drag 'em to a Revel-*Rout*:
> Then she: Behold, that Head and Hand
> Have brought to scorn the Thracian Band;
> Nor ever can our Band revive,
> While that Head, Hand, or Finger live...

Encouraged by his supporters, Handel resolved to salvage what he could of his proposed 24-night season, with revivals of *Samson*, *Saul*, *Joseph*, and a single performance of *Messiah*. On 27 March, *Belshazzar* had its première, the first of three performances. Mrs Cibber had not yet recovered, and the parts had to be redistributed, with less than satisfactory results. The piece – drawn from Biblical and Greek sources relating the last days of Jewish captivity in Babylon, and culminating in King Belshazzar's notorious feast – failed to please.

These problems did little to improve Handel's health. A friend who met him in a London street in August reported that he 'talked much of his precarious state of health, yet he looks well enough'. In the early summer, Handel is known to have visited the Earl of Gainsborough's country seat at Exton in Rutland, where he set three airs and choruses for inclusion in a private family performance of Milton's masque *Comus*. He then went on to the North Yorkshire coastal resort and spa town of Scarborough

– 'a well-built, populous and pleasant' town, according to Defoe – presumably to take the waters, which Defoe found 'tinged with a collection of mineral salts, as of vitriol, alum, iron, and perhaps sulphur'.

Towards the end of October, the Earl of Shaftesbury reported that 'Poor Handel looks something better. I hope he will entirely recover in due time, though he has been a good deal disordered in his head.' Meanwhile, England faced yet another period of strife. Taking advantage of George II's absence in Hanover during the summer, Charles Edward Stuart (Bonnie Prince Charlie), the 'Young Pretender' to the English throne, landed in Scotland in mid-July and began his march south to try to reclaim his heritage. Handel's chorus 'God save the King' (from the Coronation Anthem *Zadok the Priest*) was played everywhere; King George hastily returned to London, while the Duke of Cumberland marched northwards to do battle with the Jacobite rebels. In the new year, the King's Theatre mounted a patriotic musical drama, *La Caduta dei Giganti* (The Fall of the Giants), with music by the young German Christoph Willibald Gluck, who had been invited to London by Lord Middlesex to compose for the opera. Of the newcomer – later to write some of the finest operas of the early Classical period – Handel is said to have told Mrs Cibber, 'he knows no more of *contrapunto* than mein cook, Waltz.' Handel's own contribution to the national emergency was the *Occasional Oratorio* hastily cobbled together, largely from

Scarborough from the Castle Gate.

existing works, to celebrate the temporary retreat of the Jacobite rebels in early February 1746. The Reverend William Harris, a friend of Handel, wrote to a relative in Salisbury:

Yesterday morning I was at Handel's house to hear the rehearsal of his new occasional Oratorio. It is extremely worthy of him, which you will allow to be saying all one can in praise of it. He has but three voices for his songs – Francesina, Reinholt, and Beard; his band of music is not very extraordinary… The words of his Oratorio are scriptural, but taken from various parts, and are expressive of the rebels' flight and our pursuit of them. Had not the Duke carried his point triumphantly, this Oratorio could not have been brought on.

Jennens (who despised the librettist, Newburgh Hamilton), was openly contemptuous of the new ' "Oratorio of Shreds & patches" – 'Tis an inconceivable jumble of Milton & Spencer, a Chaos extracted from Order by the most absurd of all Blockheads, who like the Devil takes delight in defacing the Beauties of Creation… 'Tis a triumph for a Victory not yet gain'd, & if the Duke does not make hast, it may not be gain'd at the time of performance.'

In April 1746, the English forces did achieve a decisive victory at the bloody battle of Culloden. Shortly afterwards, working with a new librettist, the Reverend Thomas Morell, Handel began the oratorio *Judas Maccabaeus*. Based on the military triumphs of the eponymous Jewish hero over the barbarian Syrian hordes, *Judas Maccabaeus* was intended as a thinly-veiled homage to England's own national hero, the Duke of Cumberland. According to Morell, Handel worked at high speed, extemporising choruses at the harpsichord even before Morell could bring him the completed texts. *Judas Maccabaeus* was first performed on 1 April 1747 at the Theatre Royal in Covent Garden. With a substantial orchestra (two bassoons, two horns, three trumpets, timpani and eventually, side-drum being added to the basic complement of oboes and strings), and containing the popular air 'Come, ever-smiling Liberty' and the duet 'O lovely peace', the work was an instant success, even without the famous number 'See, the conqu'ring hero comes', which was originally written for the later oratorio *Joshua*, and subsequently transferred to *Judas Maccabaeus*. 'These oratorios of Handel's are certainly (next to the *hooting of owls*) the most solemnly striking music one can hear', wrote Catherine Talbot. 'I am sure you must be fond of them, even I am who have no ear for music, and no skill in it. In this last oratorio he has literally introduced guns [artillery kettle-drums], and they have a good effect.'

By the beginning of July, Handel had completed a 'sequel',

The battle of Culloden,
16 April 1746.

Alexander Balus – encompassing Alexander's five-year rule of the Seleucid Empire (150-145BC), his marriage to Cleopatra (not identical to Shakespeare's famous queen), and his death in battle, leaving the Israelites victorious. This was followed in mid-August by *Joshua*, a third drama of military exploits, this time of Joshua and the Israelites against Jericho and the five kingdoms. Both had texts by Morell. As an unexpected tribute to his newly-regained popularity, *Lucio Vero*, a *pasticcio* compiled from 'Airs, borrow'd entirely from Mr Handel's favourite Operas...justly styl'd the most exquisite Composition of Harmony, ever offer'd to the Publick', opened a new opera season on 14 November at the Haymarket Theatre, where Lord Middlesex was still trying to promote Italian operas to an indifferent public.

Handel's own Lenten season at Covent Garden opened on 26 February 1748 with *Judas Maccabaeus*: after three performances, Handel was able to deposit £600 in his bank account, while the first performance of *Joshua* on 9 March netted him £250, and of *Alexander Balus* on 23 March, £300. At the close of the season, he was able to purchase £4,500 worth of annuities. After many disappointments and false starts, oratorio had finally captured the public imagination. 'Will not the sedate Raptures of Oratorical Harmony attract hither an Admirer of the sublime in Music?' inquired Sir Edward Turner of an absent friend. 'Glorious Entertainment! Divine Efficacy of Music!' 'It is a vulgar

Aphorism that those who are untouched with Music, have no Souls', wrote Eliza Haywood, in her *Epistles of the Ladies*:

I was led into these Reflections by being last Night at Mr Handel's fine Oratorio of *Joshua*, where, though the Words were not quite so elegant, nor as well as I could have wished adapted to the music, I was transported into the most divine Exstasy. I closed my Eyes, and imagined myself amidst the angelic Choir, in the bright Regions of everlasting Day, chanting the praises of my great Creator, and his ineffable Messiah. I seemed, methought, to have nothing of this gross Earth about me, but was all Soul! – all Spirit!

Over the summer of 1748, Handel continued his routine of composing a pair of oratorios for the forthcoming season. As the Jacobite threat receded, martial themes, which had proved so popular under wartime conditions, were abandoned in favour of more universal subject-matter: sexual morality (*Susanna*) and justice (*Solomon*). Though the story of *Susanna* is set in Babylon, the language of the libretto and the artless charm of Handel's music, with a predominance of pastoral arias, place it unmistakably in the tradition of English ballad opera: indeed, the two lascivious Elders who seek to discredit Susanna's virtue are drawn as comic characters, whom Winton Dean has suggested represent 'the naughty old men to be found in any English village'. The Countess of Shaftesbury identified this change of style when she wrote, after attending the première on 10 February 1749: 'I cannot pretend to give my poor judgment of it from once hearing, but believe it will insinuate itself so much into my approbation as most of Handel's performances do, as it is in the light *operatic* style... I think I never saw a fuller house. Rich told me that he believed he would receive near £400.' *Solomon*, on the other hand, deals with the obligations of monarchy, presenting Solomon first as the builder of the temple and husband of a young queen; then as the proverbially wise judge, discovering the true mother of a disputed infant from the rival claims of two harlots; and finally as the philosopher king, entertaining the Queen of Sheba (the famous instrumental sinfonia which heralds her arrival is actually drawn from music by three different composers).

On 7 October 1748, the Peace of Aix-la-Chapelle finally brought the War of the Austrian Succession to an end and a grand firework display was deemed appropriate to celebrate the conclusion of hostilities. Under the direction of Giovanni Servandoni, a French theatre designer working in London, gangs of workmen laboured from November until April to erect a suitable 'machine' in Green Park. This wooden structure, 410 feet long and 114 feet high, was classical in style, with colonnades and a central triumphal arch, surmounted by a bas-relief of George II. At some point, though not by direct royal command, Handel was asked to supply music for the event. He may have found the task irksome: at any rate, his ideas differed widely from the stipulations laid down by a reluctant monarch. On 28 March 1749, a month before the ceremony was due to take place, the Duke of Montague (Master General of the Ordnance) wrote irritably to Charles Frederick ('Comptroller of his Majesty's Fireworks as well as for War as for Triumph'):

I think Hendel now proposes to have but 12 trumpets and 12 French horns; at first there was to have been sixteen of each, and I remember I told the King so, who, at that time, objected to their being any musick; but, when I told him the quantity and number of martial musick there was to be, he was better satisfied, and said he hoped there would be no fidles. Now Hendel proposes to lessen the nomber of trumpets &c. and to have violeens. I don't at all doubt but when the King hears it he will be very much displeased...

By 9 April, Handel, having compromised on the scoring – nine trumpets, nine horns, 24 oboes, 12 bassoons, a contra-bassoon (later deleted), and three pairs of kettle-drums, with strings indicated to double the oboes and bassoons – was stubbornly refusing to release his music for public rehearsal: this event (without fireworks) was announced and cancelled several times, before it finally took place at Vauxhall Gardens on 21 April, in the presence of 'the brightest and most numerous Assembly ever known at the Spring-gardens'. A crowd of 12,000 is said to have attended, causing a three-hour traffic jam on London Bridge: 'some gentlemen were wounded' in the resultant scuffles.

The grand performance itself took place as planned six days later. John Byrom described the event to his wife:

Walking about here to see sights I have retired to the stump of a tree to write a line to thee lest anything should happen to prevent me by and by...they are all mad with thanksgivings, Venetian jubilees, Italian fireworks, and German pageantry. I have before my eyes such a concourse of people as to be sure I never have or shall see again, except we should have a Peace without a vowel. The building erected on this occasion is indeed extremely neat and pretty and grand to look at, and a world of fireworks placed in an order that promises a most amazing scene when it is to be in full display. His Majesty and other great folks have been walking to see the machinery before the Queen's Library; it is all railed about there, where the lords, ladies, commons, &c. are sat under scaffolding, and seem to be under confinement in comparison of us mobility, who enjoy the free air and walks here.

It has been a very hot day, but there is a dark overcast of cloudiness which may possibly turn to rain, which occasions some of better habits

Servandoni's elaborate 'machine' for the grand firework celebration burning to the ground.

to think of retiring; and while I am now writing it spits a little and grows into a menacing appearance of rain, which, if it pass not over, will disappoint expectations. My intention, if it be fair, is to gain a post under one of the trees in St James's Park where the fireworks are in front, and where the tail of a rocket, if it should fall, cannot but be hindered by the branches from doing any mischief to them who are sheltered under them, so I shall now draw away to be ready for near shelter from either watery or fiery rain…

11 o'clock: all over, and somewhat in a hurry, by an accidental fire at one of the ends of the building, which, whether it be extinguished I know not, for I left it in an ambiguous condition that I might finish my letter, which otherwise I could not have done. I saw every fine show in front, and I believe no mischief was done by the rockets, though some pieces of above one pound and a half fell here and there…

Byrom's exit was a timely one. The firework display ended with a more spectacular conflagration than anyone had intended. Servandoni's grand pavilion burned to the ground, whereupon the distraught designer drew his sword and attacked the unfortunate 'Comptroller of his Majesty's Fireworks'. Charles Frederick fortunately sustained only minor injuries, and after a night

168

cooling his heels in a prison cell, Servandoni was 'discharg'd the next day on asking pardon before the D. of Cumberland.' George II and his royal party paid an early visit to the 'machine', and thereby escaped being roasted alive. 'The whole Band of Musick (which began to play soon after 6 o'Clock) perform'd at his Majesty's coming and going, and during his Stay in the Machine', reported the *Daily Advertiser*. No reports survive of the impression made by Handel's music, which consisted of an Overture, played before the fireworks began; three dance movements (*Bourrée*, *La Paix* and *La Réjouissance*), probably played to accompany certain allegorical fire-tableaux; and two concluding Minuets. This *Music for the Royal Fireworks*, which has since rivalled his *Water Music* in general popularity, was Handel's last ceremonial commission for the House of Hanover.

Chapter 12

'Total eclipse'

Total eclipse! no sun, no moon.
All dark amidst the blaze of noon.
Oh glorious light! no cheering ray
To glad my eyes with welcome day.
(*Samson*)

One of the greatest social evils of the eighteenth century was its treatment of children. Among the upper classes, marriages were arranged to secure the disposition of property and to provide legitimate heirs; but among the poor, casual liaisons, the lack of any effective form of birth-control, a high maternal mortality rate and overcrowded living conditions, led inevitably to the existence of thousands of unwanted infants. Many desperate, unsupported mothers abandoned their illegitimate offspring to die in the gutters; and the growing number of these pitiful little victims eventually led Thomas Coram, a retired sea-captain, to rouse public support for the foundation of a 'Hospital for the Maintenance of Exposed and Deserted Young Children'. In 1739, Coram obtained a charter and a donation from George II; subscriptions poured in from concerned individuals (including Hogarth – an artist with a social conscience), and, in 1745, the Foundling Hospital was opened on a site in Lamb's Conduit Fields (now Brunswick Square) in Bloomsbury, where it remained until the early twentieth century. The Thomas Coram Foundation still exists to help children's charities.

By 1749, only the chapel remained unfinished at the Foundling Hospital. Handel was among those who offered his services to raise money for its completion, through a concert of 'vocal and instrumental musick'. At a meeting of the General Committee on 7 May 1749, he was proposed as a Governor, an honour he finally accepted a year later. The first concert for the benefit of the Hospital took place on 27 May 1749, in the presence of the Prince and Princess of Wales and the 'young Princes and Princesses'.

The programme consisted of the 'Musick as composed for the Royal Fire-Works'; the Dettingen Anthem – with new words; selections from *Solomon*; and a new anthem specially composed for the occasion, *Blessed are They that Considereth the Poor*, which comprised pieces drawn from earlier works, together with a few original solos. 'There was no collection, but the tickets were at half a guinea, and the audience above a thousand, besides a gift of £2,000 from his majesty, and £50 from an unknown', reported the *Gentleman's Magazine*. In July, Handel commissioned his favourite organ-builder, Jonathan Morse of Barnet, to supply an organ for the chapel, which was finally completed and opened in 1753. Apart from his generosity to the Foundling Hospital, Handel continued to support many other charitable causes, ranging from a maternity hospital to the Marine Society.

During the summer of 1749, Handel completed another oratorio, *Theodora*, at his customary speed. By 8 January 1750, he

Thomas Coram

South view of the Foundling Hospital, 1749.

had also finished some incidental music for *Alceste*, a play commissioned from Tobias Smollett by Rich for his Covent Garden theatre. Although Servandoni provided scenery 'with such Magnificence... as was never exhibited in Britain before', *Alceste* was never performed. One reason may have been the series of earthquakes which struck London in February, causing the postponement of Handel's oratorio season. 'I was not under any apprehension about the earthquake, but went that night to the Oratorio, then quietly to bed...', wrote Elizabeth Montagu in March. 'The Wednesday night the Oratorio [*Judas Maccabaeus*] was very empty, though it was the most favourite performance of Handel's.'

The year of Handel's 65th birthday began auspiciously: by the end of January, he had deposited £8,000 in his bank account, and completed a new organ concerto (in G minor). On 13 February, the Earl of Shaftesbury reported that he had 'seen Handel several times...and think I never saw him so cool and well. He is quite easy in his behaviour, and has been pleasing himself in the purchase of several fine pictures, particularly a large Rembrandt, which is indeed excellent. We have scarce talked at all about musical subjects, though enough to find his performances will go off incomparably.' On 2 March, the oratorio season opened with *Saul*, followed by *Judas Maccabaeus*, and then, on 16 March, by the première of *Theodora*. The story concerns the persecution of early Christians in fourth-century Antioch: when ordered by the Roman governor to take part in pagan sacrifices, Theodora refuses and is sent to a brothel. She and another Christian convert, who is in love with her, attempt to escape, but are caught and condemned to death. *Theodora*, whose most famous air is

172

'Angels, ever bright and fair', had only three performances, attended by a very thin audience. Handel accepted its failure philosophically, saying, 'The Jews will not come to it because it is a Christian story; and the Ladies will not come, because it is a virtuous one.' According to another anecdote related by Burney, when two gentlemen applied to him, 'after the disgrace of *Theodora*, for an order to hear the MESSIAH, he cried out "Oh your sarvant, Mien-herren! you are tamnaple tainty! you would not co to TEODORA – der was room enough to tance dere, when dat was perform." '

The 1750 season ended on 12 April with a performance of *Messiah*, which had still not captured the public imagination. Within three weeks, however, Handel had organised another performance at the Foundling Hospital to inaugurate his new organ. Eager to be seen supporting a newly fashionable cause, 'an infinite croud of coaches' bore the cream of London society to hear the work; some 'Persons of Distinction' were admitted without tickets, to the disappointment of ticket-holders, who had to be turned away at the door. The first having raised over £700 for the hospital, a second performance was given on 15 May, and since that time, annual performances of *Messiah* 'fed the hungry, clothed the naked, fostered the orphan, and enriched succeeding managers of Oratorios more than any single musical production in this or any country.' (Burney). Mrs Delany's sister, Mrs Dewes, spoke for many Handelians when she wrote that:

his wonderful *Messiah* will never be out of my head; and I may say *my heart* was raised almost to heaven by it. It is only those people who have not felt the leisure of devotion that can make any objection to that performance, which is calculated to raise our devotion, and make us truly sensible of the power of the divine words he has chose beyond any human work that ever yet appeared, and I am sure I may venture to say ever will. If anything can give us an idea of the Last Day it must be that part – "The trumpet shall sound, the dead shall be raised."

On 28 July 1750, Johann Sebastian Bach died at Leipzig aged 65, having lost his sight several years before. The two greatest composers of the late Baroque had never met, although Bach apparently owned a copy of Handel's cantata *Armida abbandonata*, and had made copies of the *Brockes Passion* and the E minor *concerto grosso*. Bach's senior by one month, Handel too had intimations of mortality: at the beginning of June, he made his will, leaving several small bequests to his servants, relatives and friends (including 'my large Harpsicord, my little House Organ, my Musick Books and five hundred Pounds sterl' to his faithful amanuensis, J.C. Smith), and the bulk of his estate to his favourite niece and goddaughter, Johanna Friderika. (A codicil,

Johann Sebastian Bach
(1685-1750).

added in 1756, left additional legacies to Smith, and to two of
Handel's librettists, Morell and Newburgh Hamilton.)

During the summer, Handel travelled once more to the
Continent – either to take the waters at Aix or to visit his friends
and relatives – and apparently suffered serious injuries when his
coach overturned between The Hague and Haarlem: the *General
Advertiser* of 21 August, reported that he was 'terribly hurt [but]
is now out of Danger'. At the end of the year, Handel sent a crate
of exotic flowers and plants to the composer Telemann, an old
friend from his student days in Halle, whose passion for botany
was well-known. On New Year's Day 1751, he began a new organ
concerto in B flat (op.7 No.3), finishing it in three days; and three

Georg Philipp Telemann
(1681-1767).

weeks later, his creativity apparently undimmed, he started work
on a new oratorio. By 13 February, he had reached the chorus
'How dark, O Lord, are thy decrees' in the second part of *Jephtha*,
when he was forced to stop 'owing to weakening of the sight of my
left eye'. Ten days later, on his 66th birthday, he felt 'a little
better, and started work again', but his eye damage was permanent. On 14 March, Sir Edward Turner reported that 'Noble
Handel hath lost an eye, but I have the Rapture to say that St
Cecilia makes no complaint of any Defect in his Fingers'.

Meanwhile, the oratorio season had opened on 22 February
with *Belshazzar*, followed on 1 March by *Alexander's Feast*
coupled with a new 'musical interlude in one act titled *The Choice*

of Hercules' (which Handel had completed the previous summer with music taken from the unperformed *Alceste*). After four performances, it was succeeded by *Esther* and *Judas Maccabaeus*, before the death of the Prince of Wales on 20 March closed the theatres. In April and May, Handel directed two charity performances of *Messiah* at the Foundling Hospital, playing an organ concerto in the interval: for the second performance, there were 'above 500 coaches besides chairs &c. and the tickets amounted to above 700 guineas'. Immediately afterwards, he left to take the waters at Cheltenham, before receiving treatment from Samuel Sharp, eye-surgeon to Guy's Hospital. By the end of August, Handel managed to complete *Jephtha*, which was premièred on 26 February 1752 during his next oratorio season. Thomas Morell based his libretto loosely on an episode from the *Book of Judges*. Israel is under attack from the Ammonites, and the elders summon their half-brother Jephtha to lead them. He vows that if God gives him the victory, he, like Mozart's Idomeneo, will sacrifice the first living thing which greets him on his return. To his horror, the first person he sees is his only daughter, Iphis. In a remarkable recitative, followed by the tender air 'Waft her, angels', Jephtha prepares to fulfil his vow, but an angel appears in the nick of time with the welcome news that Iphis need only be given to God, to serve him in 'pure, angelic, virgin-state'. (This happy ending is Morell's; in the Old Testament, Jephtha's daughter dies under the knife.)

Cheltenham spa

176

Handel's health continued to deteriorate: on 17 August, the *General Advertiser* reported: 'We hear that George-Frederick Handel Esq; the celebrated Composer of Musick was seized a few Days ago with a Paralytick Disorder in his Head, which has deprived him of Sight'. On 3 November, Handel was 'couch'd' (operated on) for cataracts by William Bromfield, eye surgeon to the Prince and Princess of Wales. Mrs Delany wrote to her sister from Dublin: 'Poor Handel! how feelingly must he recollect the *"total eclipse"*... I could not help thinking with great concern of poor Handel, and lamenting his dark and melancholy circumstances; but his mind I hope will still be enlightened for the benefit of all true lovers of harmony.'

By the end of January 1753, it became clear that Handel had endured a traumatic operation (without anaesthetic) to no avail. According to a press report of 27 January: 'Mr Handel has at length, unhappily, lost his sight. Upon his being couch'd some time since, he saw so well, that his friends flattered themselves his sight was restored for a continuance; but a few days have entirely put an end to their hope.' In March, the Countess of Shaftesbury attended a performance of *Alexander's Feast*, 'but it was such a melancholy pleasure, as drew tears of sorrow, to see the great though unhappy Handel, dejected, wan, and dark, sitting by, not playing on the harpsichord, and to think how his light had been spent by *being overplied in music's cause*. I was sorry to find the audience so insipid and tasteless (I may add unkind) not to give

Interior view of the chapel at the Foundling Hospital showing the organ that Handel commissioned from Jonathan Morse of Barnet.

the poor man the comfort of applause; but affectation and conceit cannot discern or attend to merit.' This may well have been a single performance put on at the Haymarket Theatre, under the direction of John Stanley, another blind composer/organist.

Handel's own season began a few days later on 9 March with *Alexander's Feast*, and continued with *Jephtha*, *Judas Maccabaeus* and *Samson*. During April, a false rumour circulated in the press that Handel had written his own funeral anthem, to be performed after his death in the Foundling Hospital Chapel. By 10 April, the *Hallische Zeitung* had picked up the tale: 'Notwithstanding the fact that the noted Händel, this Lully of Great Britain, has had the misfortune to lose his sight, yet he, like Homer and Milton, does not allow his muse to remain idle. Perhaps the work which he now shapes will be, however, his last opus. It is to become his echo, and after his death is to be sung in the Foundling Hospital, and the profits which are earned by it he had made over to this House.' In fact, Handel had already put pen to paper for the last time, to correct a quintet added to *Jephtha* for the 1753 revival.

By 1755, Italian opera had regained some of its lost ground at the expense of Handel's oratorio seasons. Mrs Delany reported in March that the 'oratorio was miserably thin': *Joseph* and *Theodora* had single performances only. The annual *Messiah* performances at the Foundling Hospital, however, continued to attract full audiences. Mrs Delany attended in 1754, and reported that 'the music was too fine, I never heard it so well performed. The chapel is fine, and the sight of so many poor children brought up (I hope to good purpose) was a pleasant sight.' By now, the governors of the hospital evidently felt that they had proprietorial rights in *Messiah*. That year, claiming that Handel had 'given' the work to them, they petitioned Parliament to bring in a bill granting the hospital sole performance rights, except for concerts for Handel's own benefit during his lifetime. Handel denied that any such monopoly had been intended, and although he left the hospital a copy of the score and parts, he also made a similar bequest to Mercer's Hospital in Dublin.

The 1756 season proved disappointing, although Catherine Talbot wrote that the two *Messiah* nights:

made amends for the solitude of his other oratorios... The Morocco Ambassador was there [at the last *Messiah* performance on 9 April] and if his interpreter could do justice to the divine words (the music any one that has a heart must feel) how must he be affected, when in the grand choruses the whole audience solemnly rose up in joint acknowledgment that He who for our sakes *had been despised and rejected of men, was their Creator, Redeemer, King of kings, Lord of lords!*... How long even this may be fashionable I know not, for next winter there will be (if the French come) two operas; and the opera and oratorio taste are, I believe, totally incompatible.

John Taylor, the eye specialist who treated Handel.

However, though London temporarily shunned them, Handel's oratorios were gaining ground elsewhere: by 1756, they were being given regularly by musical societies not only in Dublin, but in many other British cities, including Oxford, Bath, Bristol, Hereford, Worcester and Salisbury. Performances of *Judas Maccabaeus*, *Joshua* and *Messiah* in Oxford in July 1756 were attended 'with crowded Audiences' – in contrast to the single appearance made by *Judas Maccabaeus* in the 1757 London season. Only one piece that year attracted attention: a revival of Handel's Italian oratorio *The Triumph of Time and Truth*, 'altered from the Italian [by Thomas Morell], with several new Additions'. The oratorio was revived again the following year, but Mrs Delany found 'it did not please me as usual'.

In August 1758, Handel, accompanied by Morell, visited Tunbridge Wells, where he was treated – again without success – by the eye specialist John Taylor. On 23 February 1759, a week before the opening of his final oratorio season, he celebrated his 74th birthday. The Countess of Huntingdon, an old friend, visited him during the spring. 'I have had a most pleasing interview with Handel – an interview which I shall not soon forget', she wrote. 'He is now old, and at the close of his long career; yet he is not dismayed at the prospect before him.' On 7 April, the *Whitehall Evening Post* reported: 'Last Night ended the celebrated Mr Handel's Oratorios for this Season, and the great Encouragement they have received is a sufficient Proof of their Superior Merit. He began with *Solomon*, which was exhibited twice; *Susanna* once; *Samson* three Times; *Judas Maccabaeus* twice; and the *Messiah* three Times. And this Day Mr Handel proposed setting out for Bath, to try the Benefit of the Waters, having been for some Time past in a bad State of Health.'

Handel was too weak to make the journey. According to the *Whitehall Evening Post*, he had only attended his oratorios 'with great Difficulty', and on leaving the last performance of *Messiah* on 6 April, he took to his bed. Five days later, he dictated a final codicil to his will, bequeathing, among several further remembrances to friends and servants, £1,000 to the Society for the support of Decayed Musicians and their Families, and £100 to Matthew Dubourg (such legacies ultimately accounted for almost half of his considerable estate, worth an estimated £20,000). He also took the bold and unusual step of asking permission of the Dean and Chapter of Westminster to be buried in the Abbey, and a monument ('not exceeding Six Hundred Pounds') to be raised there by his executor. A friend, James Smyth, visited him on Friday 13 April:

He took leave of all his friends on Friday morning, and desired to see

The Handel monument in
Westminster Abbey in a
copper engraving by Hanac.

nobody but the Doctor and Apothecary and myself. At 7 o'clock in the
evening he took leave of me, and told me we "should meet again"; as
soon as I was gone he told his servant "*not* to let me come to him any
more, for that he had now done with the world". He died as he lived –
a good *Christian*, with true sense of his duty to God and man, and in
perfect charity with all the world.

'This Morning, [14 April 1759] a little before Eight o'Clock
died (between 70 and 80 Years of Age) the deservedly celebrated

George Frederick Handell, Esq.', reported the *Whitehall Evening Post*, while three London papers carried a poetic eulogy:

On GEORGE FREDERICK HANDEL, Esq.
who performed in his celebrated Oratorio of
Messiah, *on the 6th, and dyed the 14th Instant.*

To melt the soul, to captivate the ear,
(Angels his melody might deign to hear)
T'anticipate on Earth the joys of Heaven,
Was Handel's task; to him the pow'r was given!
Ah! when he late attun'd Messiah's praise,
With sounds celestial, with melodious lays;
A last farewel his languid looks exprest,
And thus methinks th'enraptur'd crowd addrest:
"Adieu, my dearest friends! and also you,
"Joint sons of sacred harmony, adieu!
"Apollo, whisp'ring, prompts me to retire,
"And bids me join the bright seraphic choir!
"O for Elijah's car," great Handel cry'd;
Messiah heard his voice – and Handel dy'd.

The Dean and Chapter of Westminster Abbey acceded to the composer's last request, and on 20 April, to the accompaniment of a funeral anthem by William Croft, sung by the combined choirs of the Chapel Royal and St Paul's Cathedral, Handel's remains were interred in the south transept. The following day, the *Universal Chronicle* printed 'An Attempt towards an Epitaph', encapsulating the feelings of most music-lovers towards the departed composer:

Beneath this Place
Are reposited the Remains of
GEORGE FREDERICK HANDEL.
The most Excellent Musician
Any Age ever produced:
Whose Compositions were a
Sentimental Language
Rather than mere Sounds;
And surpassed the Power of Words
In expressing the various Passions
Of the Human Heart.

Three years later, another last request was granted when a marble statue by Roubiliac was unveiled near Poet's Corner. Inscribed simply with Handel's name and dates, it depicts the composer, pen in hand, in the process of creating his most famous aria, 'I know that my Redeemer liveth'.

Selected List of Works

Operas:
Almira (F.C. Feustking) - Hamburg, 1705
Nero (Feustking) - Hamburg, 1705
Rodrigo (F. Silvani) - Florence, 1707
Florindo (H.Hinsch) - Hamburg, 1708
Agrippina (V. Grimani) - Venice, 1709
Rinaldo (G. Rossi) - London, 1711
Il pastor fido (Rossi) - London, 1712
Teseo (N. Haym) - London, 1713
Silla (Rossi) - London, 1713
Amadigi di Gaula (Haym) - London, 1715
Radamisto (Haym) - London, 1720
Muzio Scevola (P. Rolli) - London, 1721
Floridante (Rolli) - London, 1721
Ottone (Haym) - London, 1723
Flavio (Haym) - London, 1723
Giulio Cesare (Haym) - London, 1724
Tamerlano (Haym) - London, 1724
Rodelinda (Haym) - London, 1725
Scipione (Rolli) - London, 1726
Alessandro (Rolli) - London, 1726
Admeto - London, 1727
Riccardo Primo (Rolli) - London, 1727
Siroe (Haym) - London, 1728
Tolomeo, rè di Egitto (Haym) - London, 1728
Lotario - London, 1729
Partenope - London, 1730
Poro, rè dell'Indie - London, 1731
Ezio (after Metastasio) - London, 1732
Sosarme, rè di Media - London, 1732
Orlando (after Ariosto) - London, 1733
Arianna in Creta - London, 1734
Oreste - London, 1734
Ariodante - London, 1735
Alcina - London, 1735

Atalanta - London, 1736
Arminio - London, 1737
Giustino - London, 1737
Berenice - London, 1737
Faramondo - London, 1738
Alessandro Severo - London, 1738
Serse - London, 1738
Giove in Argo - London, 1739
Imeneo - London, 1740
Deidamia (Rolli) - London, 1741

Oratorios and Odes:
Il trionfo del Tempo e del Disinganno (B. Pamphili) - Rome, 1707
La resurrezione (C.S. Capece) - Rome, 1708
Ode for the Birthday of Queen Anne (? A. Philips) - Windsor or
    London, 1713
Der für die Sünde der Welt gemartete und sterbende Jesus (B.H. Brockes)
    - ? Hamburg, 1716
Acis and Galatea (J. Gay et al) - Cannons, 1718; London, 1732
Esther (Pope and Arbuthnot) - Cannons, ?1718; London, 1732
Deborah (Humphreys) - London, 1733
Athaliah (Humphreys) - Oxford, 1733
Il Parnasso in festa - London, 1734
Alexander's Feast (Dryden) - London, 1736
Il trionfo del Tempo e della Verità (Pamphili) - London, 1737
Saul (C. Jennens) - London, 1739
Israel in Egypt - London, 1739
Ode for St Cecilia's Day (Dryden) - London, 1739
L'Allegro, il Penseroso ed il Moderato (Jennens, after Milton) -
    London, 1740
Messiah (Jennens) - Dublin, 1742
Samson (N. Hamilton, after Milton) - London, 1743
Semele (W. Congreve) - London, 1744
Joseph and his Brethren (J. Miller) - London, 1744
Hercules (T. Broughton) - London, 1745
Belshazzar (Jennens) - London, 1745
Occasional Oratorio (Hamilton) - London, 1746
Judas Maccabaeus (T. Morell) - London, 1747
Joshua (Morell) - London, 1748
Alexander Balus (Morell) - London, 1748
Susanna - London, 1749
Solomon - London, 1749
Theodora (Morell) - London, 1750
The Choice of Hercules (R. Lowth) - London, 1751
Jephtha (Morell) - London, 1752
The Triumph of Time and Truth (Morell) - London, 1757

Sacred vocal:

Carmelite Vespers - Rome, 1707
- *Dixit Dominus* (psalm)
- *Laudate Pueri* (psalm)
- *Te decus virgineum* (antiphon)
- *Nisi Dominus* (psalm)
- *Haec est regina virginum* (antiphon)
- *Saeviat tellus* (antiphon)
- *Salve regina* (antiphon)

Chandos Anthems - Cannons, 1717-18
- *As Pants the Hart*
- *Have Mercy upon Me, O God*
- *In the Lord put I my Trust*
- *I will Magnify Thee, O God*
- *Let God Arise*
- *My Song shall be Alway*
- *O be Joyful* (Chandos *Jubilate*)
- *O Come let us Sing unto the Lord*
- *O Praise the Lord with one Consent*
- *O Sing unto the Lord*
- *The Lord is my Light*

Coronation Anthems - Westminster Abbey, 1727
- *Let thy Hand be Strengthened*
- *The King shall Rejoice*
- *My Heart is Inditing*
- *Zadok the Priest*

Other anthems:
As Pants the Hart (3 settings)
Blessed are They that Considereth the Poor (Foundling Hospital Anthem)
How Beautiful are the Feet (Anthem on the Peace, 1749)
I will Magnify Thee, O God
Let God Arise
O Sing unto the Lord
Sing unto God (for wedding of Prince of Wales, 1736)
The King shall Rejoice (Dettingen Anthem, 1743)
The Ways of Zion do Mourn (for funeral of Queen Caroline, 1737)
This is the Day (for wedding of Princess Anne, 1734)
Utrecht Te Deum (1713)
Utrecht Jubilate (1713)
'Caroline' Te Deum (1714)
Chandos Te Deum (c.1718)
Dettingen Te Deum (1743)

Secular vocal:

7 dramatic Italian cantatas
24 solo and duet Italian cantatas with instruments
71 solo Italian cantatas with *continuo*
22 Italian duets and trios with *continuo*

Many English songs
6 Italian songs
9 French songs
14 German arias

Orchestral:

Water Music (3 instrumental suites, in F, D and G) (?1717)
[6] *Concerto grossi*, op.3 (London, 1734)
6 Concertos [for organ], op.4 (London, 1738)
A Second Set of Six Concertos [for organ] (London, 1740)
12 Grand Concertos in 7 parts, op.6 (London, 1740)
3 Concerti a due cori (1748)
Music for the Royal Fireworks (1749)
A Third Set of Six Concertos [for organ], op.7 (London, 1761)
Miscellaneous overtures, sinfonias and dances
Miscellaneous marches and minuets for wind ensemble

Instrumental:

15 solo sonatas, including 12 Sonatas for treble instrument and
  continuo, op.1 (London, c.1730)
18 trio sonatas, including 6 Sonatas for 2 treble instruments and
  continuo, op.2 (London, c.1780); 7 Sonatas or Trios, for 2 violins/
  flutes and *continuo*, op.5 (London, 1739)

Keyboard:

8 Suites de pièces pour le clavecin (London, 1720)
[9] *Suites de pièces pour le clavecin* ii (London, 1733)
Numerous other individual movements, sonatas, etc.

Selected Bibliography

Abraham, Gerald, ed.: *Handel: A Symposium*, London, 1954

Addison, Joseph: Articles in *The Spectator* (1710-12)
   Remarks on Several Parts of Italy &c. In the Years 1701, 1702, 1703, London, 1705

Burney, Charles: *A General History of Music from the Earliest Ages to the Present Period*, London, 1776-89, repr. 1957
   An Account of the Musical Performances in Westminster Abbey and the Pantheon...in Commemoration of Handel, London, 1785, repr. 1965
   An 18th-Century Musical Tour in France and Italy, London, 1770, repr. 1959
   An 18th-Century Musical Tour in Central Europe and the Netherlands, London, 1770, repr. 1959

Dean, Winton: *Handel and the Opera Seria*, London, 1970
   Handel's Dramatic Oratorios and Masques, London, 1959
   'Handel', *The New Grove Dictionary of Music and Musicians*, London, 1980

Defoe, D: *A Tour through the Whole Island of Great Britain (1724-6)*, repr. 1971

Dent, Edward J.: *Handel*, London, 1934

Deutsch, Otto Erich: *Handel: A Documentary Biography*, London, 1955

Dixon, Graham:'Handel's Carmelite Vespers' CD booklet for EMI recording by Taverner Choir, 1989

Fiske, Roger: *English Theatre Music in the 18th Century*, London, 1973

Harris, Ellen: *Handel and the Pastoral Tradition*, London, 1980

Hawkins, Sir John: *A General History of the Science and Practice of Music*, London, 1776, repr. 1963

Hogwood, Christopher: *Handel*, London, 1984

Kirkendale, Ursula: 'The Ruspoli Documents on Handel', *Journal of the American Musicological Society*, xvii (1964), 170

Lang, Paul Henry: *George Frideric Handel*, New York, 1966, repr. 1977

Larsen, Jens Peter: *Handel's Messiah: Origins, Composition, Sources*, London, 1957

Mainwaring, John: *Memoirs of the Life of the Late George Frederic Handel*, London, 1760, repr. 1967

Mattheson, J: *Georg Friedrich Handels Lebensbeschreibung*, Hamburg, 1761, repr. 1976

Grundläge einer Ehren-Pforte, Hamburg, 1740

The New Oxford History of Music, v (*Opera and Church Music, 1630-1750*)

Porter, Roy: *English Society in the Eighteenth Century*, London, 1982

Sadie, Stanley: *Handel*, London, 1962

Handel Concertos, London, 1972

Shaw, Watkins: *A Textual and Historical Companion to Handel's Messiah*, London, 1965

Trevelyan, G.M.: *English Social History*, London, 1944, repr. 1980

Wilson, ed.: *Roger North on Music*, London, 1959

Young, Percy: *Handel*, London, 1946

Acknowledgements and References

The Author gratefully acknowledges her debt to many sources - listed in the Bibliography - and also to Naomi Saxl for all her help and encouragement.

All pictures from Archiv für Kunst und Geschichte, Berlin, except: Mary Evans Picture Library pp. 9, 17, 18, 24, 51, 53, 62, 65, 65, 69, 71, 76, 89, 113, 117, 129, 132, 136, 171, 172, 174, 177, 179

Hulton Deutsch Collection Ltd. pp. 6, 38, 39, 45, 48, 54, 56, 60, 64, 72, 75, 77, 78, 79, 82, 100, 101, 104, 107, 113, 118, 121, 122, 131, 133, 147, 148, 158, 163, 165, 168, 176

Index

*Page numbers in **bold** refer to illustrations*

Anne, Queen of England **48**, 49, 51, 52, 66, 68
Arbuthnot, John 65, 66, 79, 81, 84, 86
Ariosti, Attilio 21, 22, 87, 89, 90, 96, 110
Arne, Thomas Sr. 16, 108, 118, 138, 149, 152

Bach, Johann Sebastian 7, 12, 27, 71, 141, 173, 174, **174**
Baldassari, Benedetto 84
Banister, John 56, 57, 58
Barberini, Cardinals Antonio and Francesco 36, **36**
Beard, John 117, 154, 160, 164
Beethoven, Ludwig van 9, 12
[*The*] *Beggar's Opera* 99, **100**, **101**, 147
Bernacchi, Antonio 104, 105
Berselli, Matteo 84, 86
Betterton, Thomas 54, 55
Blow, John 52, 59
Bononcini, Giovanni Battista 21, 22, **22**, 55, 56, 84, 87, 88, 89, 90, 95, 96, 97, 108
Bordoni, Faustina 92, 94, **94**, 95, 96, 97, 99, 100, 102, 104, 144
Boyce, William 138
Boyle, Richard, Earl of Burlington 65, 70, 83, 84
Broughton, Rev. Thomas 160
Burlington, Earl of [see Boyle, Richard]
Buxtehude, Dietrich 27
Brydges, James [see First Duke of Chandos]
Byrom, John 88, 167, 168

Caffarelli [see Majorelli]
Carestini, Giovanni 114, 116, 118, 120, 122, 123,
Carey, Henry 136, **136**
Castrucci, Domenico and Pietro 39
Chandos, First Duke of 77, 78, **78**, 79, 80, 83, 107, 135
Cibber, Susanna 128, 149, 150, 152, 154, 160, 161, 163
Clarke, Jeremiah 52, 59, 120
Clayton, Thomas 63
Congreve, William 55, 87
Conti, Gioacchino 122, 123, 124, 143
Coram, Thomas 170, 171, **171**
Corelli, Arcangelo 10, 37, 38, **38**, 40, 44, 141, 146,
Croft William 52, 181
Cuzzoni, Francesca 89, **89**, 90, 92, 93, 94, 95, 96, 97, 99, 100, 105, 110, 114, 143, 144

Davenant, Sir William 53, 55
Delany, Mary [see Pendarves]
Dieupart, Charles 63
Dubourg, Matthew 123, 147, 148, 149, 154, 155, 179
Duparc, Elisabeth 135
Durastante, Margherita 39, 41, 44, 84, 86, 87

Eccles, John 52
Épine, Margharita de l' 64

Farinelli 104, 110, 115, 116, **116**, 118, 119, 120, 143, 144
Faustina [see Bordoni]
Ferdinando, Prince 30, 33, 34

Galerati, Catterina 84
Galuppi, Baldassare 146
Garrick, David 152, **152**
Gay, John 65, **65**, 73, 81, 88, 90, 99
George I, King of England [formerly Elector of Hanover] 46, 68, 69, **69**, 70, 71, 72, 74, 75, 76, 77, 77, 83, 85, 97
George II, King of England 97, **98**, 99, 105, 106, 115, 141, 157, 163, 167, 169, 170
George III, King of England 7, 74, 121, 122, 123, 125
Gerstenbüttel, Joachim 24, 25
Gismondi, Celeste 110
Gizziello [see Conti]
Gluck, Christoph Willibald 163
Greene, Dr Maurice 131, **131**, 138
Grimaldi, Niccolò 61, 70, 87

Hamilton, Newburgh 164, 174
Händel, Georg l, 13, **14**, 15, 16, 17
Handel, George Frideric **58**, **67**, **77**, **82**, **126**, **129**, **132**, **138**, **180**
Aci, Galatea, e Polifemo 42
Acis and Galatea 9, 42, **80**, 81, 106, 108, 109, 110, 113, 114, 141, 149, 150
Admeto 96, 99, 106
Agrippina 44, 64, 84, 133
Alceste 172, 176
Alcina 119, 120, 123
Allessandro 93, 95, 110, 158
Allessandro Severo 136
Alexander Balus 165
Alexander's Feast 9, 120, 121, 124, 137, 140, 141, 150, 175, 177, 178
Almira 28, 29, 30, 60
Amadigi 68, 69, 70, 76
Arianna in Creta 114, 117
Ariodante 118, 119, 122
Armida abbandonata 40, 173
Arminio 123
As pants the Hart 136
Atalanta 122, 123, 146

Athaliah 113, 114, 119
Belshazzar 160, 161, 162, 175
Berenice 124
Blessed are They that Considereth the Poor 171
Brockes Passion 173
Cajo Fabricio 114
Chandos Anthems 79, 81, 161
[The] Choice of Hercules 176
Concerti grossi 140, 141, 149, 173
Coronation Anthems 97
Deborah 111, 112, 113, 119, 124, 136, 149, 161
Deidamia 143
Dettingen Te Deum 157
Diana cacciatrice 40
Didone abbandonata 124
Dixit Dominus 39
Dorinda 64
Esther 81, 107, 108, 109, 110, 113, 119, 124, 149, 150, 176
Ezio 106
Faramondo 135
Flavio 90
Floridante 88
Florindo 29, 30
From harmony 9, 141, 145, 150
Giove in Argo 140
Giulio Cesare 90, **91**, 105, 106
Giustino 123
Haec est regina virginem 39
[The] Harmonious Blacksmith 12, 85
Hendel, non può mia Musa 40
Hercules 160, 161
Il Parnasso in festa 114
Il pastor fido 63, 115, 116, 117
Il trionfo del Tempo e del Disinganno 37, 38
Il trionfo del Tempo e della Verità 124, 140, 179
Imeneo 143, 150
Israel in Egypt 12, 139, 140
Jephtha 175, 176, 178
Joseph and his Brethren 159, 162, 178
Joshua 9, 12, 164, 165, 166, 179
Jubilate 68

Judas Maccabaeus 164, 165, 172, 176, 178, 179
[The] King shall Rejoice 97, 157
L'Allegro, il Penseroso ed il Moderato 141, 143, 145, 149, 150
Laudate pueri 39
Let thy Hand be Strengthened 97
Lucretia 40
Messiah 7, 8, 9, 12, 140, 150, 151, **151**, 152, 155, **155**, 156,157, 160, 162, 173, 176, 178, 179, 181
Music for the Royal Fireworks 12, 169, 171
Muzio Scevola 87, 88, 133
My Heart is Inditing 97
Nero 29
Nisi Dominus 39
O be Joyful 80
Occasional Oratorio 163
Oreste 118
Organ concertos 149, 150, 154, 172, 174
Orlando 110
Ottone 83, 89, 90, 114, 118
Partenope 105, 106
Poro 105, 106, 123
Radamisto 84, 87
[La]resurrezione 40
Riccardo Primo 99
Rinaldo 29, 60, 71, 76, 99, 106
Rodelinda 92, 93, 106
Rodrigo 34, 35, 40
Rossane [see Alessandro]
Saeviat tellus 39
Salve regina 39
Samson 154, 155, 156, 159, 161, 162, 170, 178, 179
Saul 139, 140, 152, 159, 162, 172
Scipione 95, 105
Semele 157, 158, 159, 160
Semiramide riconosciuto 114
Serse 135, 136
Silla 68
Sing unto God 121
Siroe 99, 100
Solomon 166, 171, 179
Sosarme, rè di Medea 106, 115
Susanna 166, 179

Tamerlano 92, 106
Te decus virginem 39
Te deum 68, 69, 81
Terpiscore 117
Teseo 64
Theodora 131, 171, 172, 173, 178
This is the Day 115
Tolomeo, rè di Egitto 99, 102, 110
Trio sonatas, Op. 5 140
Utrecht Jubilate 80, 114, 148, 149
Utrecht Te Deum 114, 148, 149
Venus and Adonis 63
Water Music 12, 69, **70**, 76, 121, 169
[The] Ways of Zion do Mourn 135
Zadok the Priest 97, 163
Hanover, Elector of [see George I]
Hasse, Johann 10, 115, 120, 143, 146
Haydn, Franz Joseph 9
Haym, Nicola Francesco 63, 64, 70, 90, 94
Heidegger, John Jacob 60, **60**, 65, 75, 83, 84, 103, 104, 106, 108, 110, 111, 115, 135, 138, 143

Jennens, Charles 132, 139, 141, 142, 149, 150, 151, 153, 156, 157, 160, 164

Keiser, Reinhard 10, 25, 28, 29, 71
Kielmansegge, Baron 45, 46, 68, 75
Killigrew, Thomas 53
Kusser, Sigismund 25, 147

Lottini, Antonio 135
Louis XIV, King of France 24, 49, 51, 66, 79
Lully, Jean-Baptiste 10, **11**, 24, 25, 60, 64, 70, 96, 110

Majorelli, Gaetano 135, 136
Marchesini, Maria 135
Marlborough, John, First Duke of 49, **50**, 77, 88

Mattheson, Johann 25, **26**, 27, 28, 29, 71, 125, 133
Mendelssohn, Felix 10
Milton, John 141, 142, **142**, 154, 159, 164
Monteverdi, Claudio 42
Morell, Rev. Thomas 131, 164, 165, 174, 176, 179
Mozart, Wolfgang Amadeus 9, 46, 130, 176

Neale, John and William, Publisher 147

Ottoboni, Cardinal Pietro 36, 37, 38

Paisible, James 52
Pamphili, Cardinal Benedetto 36, 37, 40, 132
Pellegrini, Valeriano 44, 64
Pendarves, Mary [later Delany] 87, 95, 99, 105, 115, 119, 123, 127, 143, 158, 159, 173, 177, 178, 179
Pepusch, John Christopher 57, 79, **79**, 99, 138
Pilotti 64, 70
Pope, Alexander 65, 66, **66**, 73, 81, 107
Prussia, Friedrich I, King of **20**, 21
Purcell, Henry 10, 51, 55, **55**, 59, 66, 67, 80

Quantz, Johann Joachim 87, 96, 97

Rich, Christopher 54, 55, 56
Robinson, Anastasia 70, **71**, 84
Rolli, Paolo 83, 84, 85, 86, 87, 104, 105, 112, 114, 116
Roubiliac, Louis François 73, 136, 137, **138**, 181
Ruspoli, Marquis Francesco Maria di 39, 40, 41, 42, 87

Sallé, Marie 10, 117, **117**, 118, 120
Savage, William 135
Saxe-Weissenfels, Duke of 16, 17, 18, **18**
Scarlatti, Alessandro 10, 33, 38, 44, 84
Scarlatti, Domenico 33, 38, 43
Scheidt, Samuel 14, 15
Senesino, Bernardi Francesco 83, 84, 86, 87, 90, 92, 93, 94, 95, 96, 99, 100, 103, 104, 105, 106, 108, 109, 110, 112, 114, 116, 120, 123, 143, 144
Servandoni, Giovanni 166, 167, **167**, 168, 169
Smith, John Christopher [formerly Johann Christoph Schmidt] 15, 71
Smith, John Christopher Jr. 71, 173
Steffani, Agostino 46
Strada, Anna 104, 105, 106, 108, 109, 110, 112, 114, 118, 119, 120, 122, 124, 127, 135, 136, 143
Swift, Jonathan 73, 90, 131, 152, 153, **153**

Tarquini, Vittoria 34, 125
Taylor, John 179, **179**
Telemann, Georg Philipp 71, 174, **175**
Tyers, Jonathan 136, 137, 138, 141

Urbani, Valentino 61

Wagner, Richard 12
Walpole, Robert, Sir 111, **111**, 112, 141
Walsh, John, Publisher 61, 62, **80**, 106, 137, 140, 141

Zachow, Friedrich Wilhelm 18, 47

3/96 (23669)